STECK-VAUGHN   BOOK ONE ★ TO

AMERICA'S STORY

BY VIVIAN BERNSTEIN

STECK-VAUGHN
C O M P A N Y
Elementary • Secondary • Adult • Library

✎★ ABOUT THE AUTHOR

Vivian Bernstein is the author of *World History and You, World Geography and You, American Government,* and *Decisions for Health.* She received her Master of Arts degree from New York University. Bernstein is active with professional organizations in social studies, education, and reading. She gives presentations to school faculties and professional groups about content area reading. Bernstein was a teacher in the New York City Public School System for a number of years.

✎★ ACKNOWLEDGMENTS

Executive Editor: Diane Sharpe
Senior Editor: Martin S. Saiewitz
Design Manager: Richard Balsam
Designer: Pamela Heaney
Photo Editor: Margie Foster
Electronic Production: Shelly M. Knapp
Cover Production: Claunch Consulting

✎★ CREDITS

Cover Photography: Reagan Bradshaw Photography

Photo Credits: pp. 2–3, 4, 5, 6 The Granger Collection; p. 10 The Bettmann Archive; p. 11a & b The Granger Collection; p. 11c North Wind Picture Archives; p. 15 The Granger Collection; p. 16a The Bettmann Archive; pp. 16b, 17 North Wind Picture Archives; pp. 20, 21, 22, 25, 26, 27a & b The Granger Collection; p. 27c The Bettmann Archive; p. 31 The Granger Collection; p. 32a The Bettmann Archive; pp. 32b & c, 33 The Granger Collection; p. 34 North Wind Picture Archives; pp. 38–39, 40, 41a The Granger Collection; p. 41b © Uniphoto; p. 41c North Wind Picture Archives; p. 42 The Granger Collection; pp. 43, 46 The Bettmann Archive; p. 47a & c The Granger Collection; p. 47b Reagan Bradshaw; p. 48a The Valentine Museum; pp. 48b, 49a The Granger Collection; p. 49b The Bettmann Archive; p. 52 The Granger Collection; p. 53a Reagan Bradshaw; p. 53b © Uniphoto; p. 54a Reagan Bradshaw; p. 54b © Henryk T. Kaiser/Photri; p. 54c © Uniphoto; p. 55a © Keith Jewel; p. 55b © Bob Daemmrich/Uniphoto; p. 58 The Bettmann Archive; pp. 59, 60 The Granger Collection; p. 63 The Bettmann Archive; p. 64a The Granger Collection; p. 64b © Uniphoto; pp. 65, 66a The Granger Collection; p. 66b North Wind Picture Archives; pp. 70–71, 72 The Granger Collection; p. 73a The Bettmann Archive; p. 73b North Wind Picture Archives; p. 73c The Granger Collection; p. 74 Courtesy The Missouri Historical Society; pp. 75, 79, 80 The Granger Collection; p. 81a North Wind Picture Archives; pp. 81b, 82, 85, 86, 87a, 88a The Granger Collection; p. 88b North Wind Picture Archives; p. 92 Mount Holyoke College Art Museum, South Hadley, MA; p. 93a The Granger Collection; p. 93b North Wind Picture Archives; p. 94 The Granger Collection; pp. 98–99 Courtesy The Bucks County Historical Society, Doylestown, PA; pp. 100, 101a North Wind Picture Archives; p. 102a & b Courtesy The Institute for Texan Cultures; p. 102c The Granger Collection; p. 102d © Quinn Stewart; p. 103a Courtesy The Institute for Texan Cultures; p. 103b The Granger Collection; p. 103c Courtesy The Barker Texas History Center, University of Texas, Austin; p. 106 Courtesy Texas State Archives; p. 107a The Bettmann Archive; p. 107b The Granger Collection; pp. 109, 113 North Wind Picture Archives; pp. 115, 116 The Granger Collection; p. 119 The Bettmann Archive; p. 120 The Granger Collection; p. 121a North Wind Picture Archives; p. 121b The Granger Collection; p. 122a The Bettmann Archive; pp. 122b, 125 The Granger Collection; p. 126a © Quinn Stewart; pp. 126b, 127a The Granger Collection; p. 127b Courtesy The Sophia Smith Collection, Smith College; p. 128a The Bettmann Archive; p. 128b The Granger Collection.

Cartography: Maryland CartoGraphics

Cover artifacts: Courtesy of Richard Balsam, Reagan Bradshaw, Charles Bunn, Carey Collier, Michael and Pamela Heaney, Karen Hurley, Tim Knapp, Yolanda Rodriguez, Diane Sharpe, Rochelle Storin.

CONTENTS

America's Story tells the story of our country. Our country is the United States of America. This book tells how our country became a land of freedom. It tells how the United States changed from a small country to a very large one.

Our country's story began with Native Americans. Later, people who came to America from Great Britain started 13 colonies. These colonies were ruled by Great Britain.

As time passed, people in the American colonies wanted to be free from British rule. They fought and won a war against the British. After the war, the colonies became a free country. This country was called the United States of America. The leaders of the new United States wrote laws. Those laws protected the freedom of the people.

At first, the United States had only 13 states. Slowly the country grew larger. Americans moved west. More and more states became part of the United States.

As the country grew, problems between the northern and southern states also grew. People in the North and in the South disagreed about slavery. Some southern states decided to leave the United States. They started a new nation. This led to a long, terrible war. After the war, the United States became one nation again.

For more than two hundred years, people have worked to make our country a land of freedom. As you read this book, you will learn how many kinds of Americans have built this country. Read on to learn about the men and women who were part of America's story.

THE SETTLERS OF AMERICA

What do you think it was like to go across an ocean hundreds of years ago? You would not see land for many days. No one would come to help you if you lost your way. You might get sick. Rats might eat the food on your ship. Yet hundreds of years ago, brave people took this dangerous trip to come to America.

About 500 years ago, people from Europe started coming to America. People came to America for different reasons. Some came to find gold. Others came because they wanted more freedom. Many people from Europe stayed to live in America. The Pilgrims came to live in America. But the people from Europe were not the first to live in America. Native Americans had been living in America for thousands of years. Some Native Americans helped settlers like the Pilgrims live in America.

How did Native Americans live their lives? Who were the people from Europe who explored and settled in America? As you read Unit 1, think about why different groups of people made the dangerous trip to America.

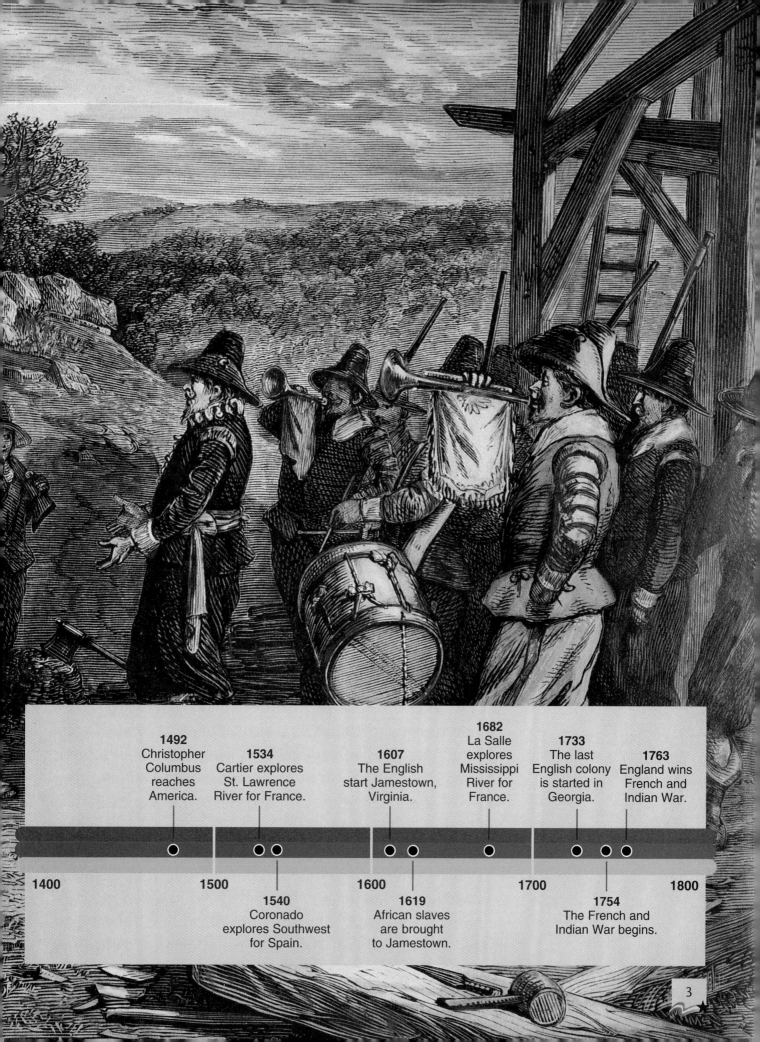

1492
Christopher Columbus reaches America.

1534
Cartier explores St. Lawrence River for France.

1607
The English start Jamestown, Virginia.

1682
La Salle explores Mississippi River for France.

1733
The last English colony is started in Georgia.

1763
England wins French and Indian War.

1400   1500   1600   1700   1800

1540
Coronado explores Southwest for Spain.

1619
African slaves are brought to Jamestown.

1754
The French and Indian War begins.

CHAPTER 1

THE FIRST AMERICANS

Native Americans of the Northwest sometimes used nets to catch fish.

Think About As You Read

1. How did Native Americans live long ago?
2. Why did Native Americans live differently in different parts of the United States?
3. What have other people learned from Native Americans?

NEW WORDS

religions
cotton
buffalo

PEOPLE & PLACES

Native Americans
America
Asia
United States of America
United States
Northwest
Southwest
Midwest
Great Plains
East

Native Americans were the first people to live in America. They may have lived in Asia before coming to this land. Native Americans are also known as Indians. They settled in different parts of America. Native Americans lived here for thousands of years. Then people from other lands started coming to America. About 220 years ago the name of our country became the United States of America. Native Americans lived in this land long before it was called the United States.

Native Americans in different parts of the United States spoke different languages. They also lived in different kinds of houses. They wore different kinds of clothes. They ate different kinds of food. They believed in different **religions**.

Many Native Americans lived in the Northwest of the United States. In the Northwest, there were thick forests. There were many fish in the ocean and rivers. The Native Americans of the Northwest went fishing to get food. They ate fish every day. They built houses and boats from trees in the forests.

Some Native Americans lived in the Southwest. In the Southwest, there was little rain. There were few trees. There were very few fish and animals to eat. The Native Americans of the Southwest became farmers. They used river water to grow food. They grew corn and beans for food. They also grew **cotton**. They made their clothes from cotton.

In the Midwest of the United States the land is very flat. We call this flat land the Great Plains. Millions of **buffalo** lived on the Great Plains. Many Native Americans lived on the Great Plains. They became buffalo hunters. They used every part of the buffalo that were killed. They ate buffalo meat. They made clothes out of buffalo skins. They lived in tents that were made of buffalo skins.

In the East of the United States there were many forests. Animals lived in the forests. Many Native Americans lived in these forests. They became hunters. They killed deer and turkeys for food. They also became farmers. They grew corn, pumpkins, and beans for their families.

Regions of the United States

Baskets made by Native Americans in the East

Native Americans who lived on the Great Plains hunted buffalo.

Native Americans who lived on the Great Plains made tents out of buffalo skins.

There were some ways that all Native Americans were alike. They loved beautiful plants and animals. They took good care of their land.

All Native Americans made their own tools. They needed tools for hunting, farming, and fishing. Native Americans made their tools out of stones and animal bones. They did not make metal tools. They made knives out of stones. Native Americans hunted with bows and arrows. They did not have guns.

Native Americans taught many things to people who later came to America. They taught them how to plant new foods like corn and potatoes. They taught people how to use special plants for medicine. Native American medicines helped sick people get well.

There are many Native Americans in the United States today. They still enjoy many songs, dances, and stories that their people enjoyed long ago. But Native Americans now work at many kinds of jobs. There are Native American doctors and teachers. Some Native Americans are farmers and builders. Native Americans today are proud that they were the first people to build our country. They are proud that they were the first Americans.

★ Read and Remember

Finish Up   Choose a word in blue print to finish each sentence. Write the word on the correct blank.

Americans	fishing	medicines
corn	buffalo	hunters

1. Native Americans were the first _____ .

2. Native Americans who lived in the Northwest went _____ for their food.

3. The Native American farmers of the Southwest grew beans and

   _____ .

4. Animals that lived on the Great Plains were the _____ .

5. Native Americans who lived on the Great Plains became _____ .

6. Native Americans used special plants to make _____ .

Think and Apply ★

Fact or Opinion   A **fact** is a true statement. An **opinion** is a statement that tells what a person thinks.

> **Fact**   The land is very flat in the Midwest.
> **Opinion**   The Midwest is the best place to live.

Write **F** next to each fact below. Write **O** next to each opinion. You should find two sentences that are opinions.

_____ 1. Native Americans spoke different languages.

_____ 2. Millions of buffalo lived on the Great Plains.

_____ 3. It was easy to live on the Great Plains.

_____ 4. Native Americans made tools from stones and bones.

_____ 5. The best tools were made from stones.

Journal Writing

Think about the different groups of Native Americans. Choose two groups. Write about where they lived. Then tell how they got food. Write four to six sentences in your journal.

Crossword Puzzle

Each sentence below has a word missing. Choose the missing word for each sentence from the words in blue print. Then write the words in the correct places on the puzzle.

─────────────── **ACROSS** ───────────────

stores farmers Southwest stone

1. Native Americans knives were made of _____ .

2. People who grow vegetables for food are _____ .

3. Native Americans of the _____ grew cotton so they could make clothes.

4. Native Americans did not have _____ where they could buy things.

─────────────── **DOWN** ───────────────

arrow bones hunter metal

5. Native Americans did not make _____ tools.

6. Native Americans made tools out of stone and animal _____ .

7. A Native American who killed animals for food was a _____ .

8. The Native American hunter used a bow and _____ .

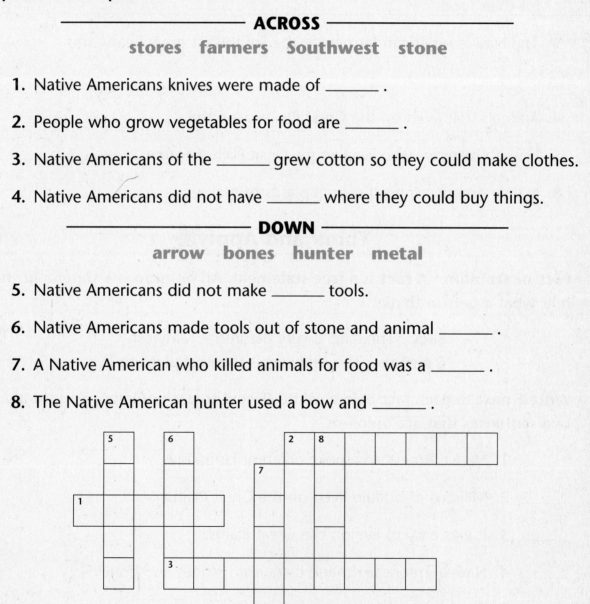

Skill Builder

Understanding Continents   We live on the Earth. The Earth has large bodies of land called **continents**. There are seven continents. Most continents have many countries. We live on the continent of North America. Our country, the United States, is in North America.

Here is a list of the continents in order of their size. The largest continent is first on the list.

1. Asia
2. Africa
3. North America
4. South America
5. Antarctica
6. Europe
7. Australia

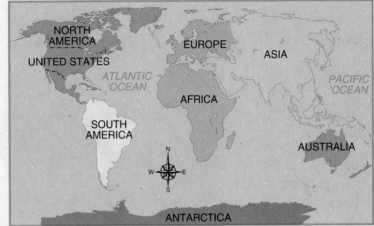

Look at the map above. Write a sentence to answer each question.

1. What are the seven continents? _____

   _____

   _____

2. Which continent has the United States? _____

   _____

3. Which is the largest continent? _____

   _____

4. Which is the smallest continent? _____

   _____

5. Which ocean separates North America from Africa and Europe? _____

   _____

After sailing for many days, Christopher Columbus and his crew reached an island in America.

Christopher Columbus lived a long time ago. Columbus was born in 1451 in Italy. Columbus became a sailor. He also made maps.

In the 1400s, people knew less about the world than we know today. Some people believed the world was flat. No one in Europe knew there was the land we now call America. Only the Native Americans knew about their land.

At that time, people from Europe went to India to get jewels, silks, and **spices**. They traveled thousands of miles to the east to reach India. Their route was long and dangerous.

Christopher Columbus

Christopher Columbus wanted to find an easier way to travel to India. Christopher Columbus thought the world was round. He believed he could go to India by sailing west across the Atlantic Ocean.

Many people did not believe Columbus. They laughed at him.

Columbus needed ships and sailors to sail across the Atlantic Ocean. Columbus went to see Isabella, the queen of Spain. Queen Isabella thought about Columbus's plan for six years. She believed he was right. She thought Columbus could reach India by sailing across the Atlantic Ocean. She wanted Columbus to find gold for Spain. So Queen Isabella decided to help him.

Queen Isabella gave Columbus three small ships. The names of the ships were the *Niña*, the *Pinta*, and the *Santa Maria*.

Queen Isabella

Columbus sailed with three ships—the *Niña*, the *Pinta*, and the *Santa Maria*.

11

Columbus and the sailors sailed west across the Atlantic Ocean. For many days the sailors could not see land. Many sailors were afraid. The sailors said, "Turn back for Spain, Columbus." Columbus was braver than the sailors. Columbus said, "I will not turn back. We will sail until we reach India."

On October 12, 1492, the sailors had not seen land for 33 days. On that day the three ships reached an island. The sailors were no longer afraid.

Columbus thought he was in India. He was not in India. Columbus was on an American island. People already lived on this island. Columbus called these people Indians because he thought he was in India. Now Indians are known as Native Americans.

Columbus **claimed** America for Spain. For the people of Europe, America was a **New World**. Of course, it was not a new world to the Native Americans who lived there. Soon after Columbus's trip, more people from Europe would come to America.

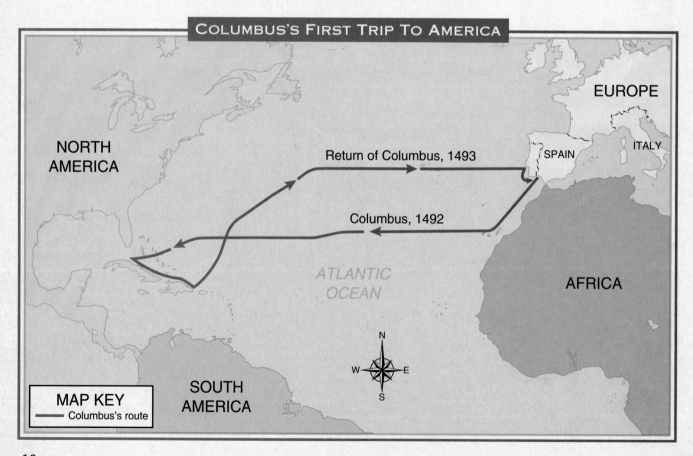

COLUMBUS'S FIRST TRIP TO AMERICA

EUROPE

NORTH AMERICA

Return of Columbus, 1493

SPAIN

ITALY

Columbus, 1492

ATLANTIC OCEAN

AFRICA

N
W   E
S

MAP KEY
— Columbus's route

SOUTH AMERICA

Read and Remember

Circle the Answer   Draw a circle around the correct answer.

1. Where did Columbus want to go?
   America   India   Europe

2. Why did people from Europe want to go to India?
   to travel   to get jewels, silks, and spices   to see buffalo

3. What did Queen Isabella give to Columbus?
   jewels   ships   spices

4. What ocean did Columbus sail across?
   Pacific Ocean   Indian Ocean   Atlantic Ocean

5. When did Columbus reach America?
   1412   1451   1492

6. What did Columbus call the people he found in America?
   Indians   Americans   Asians

7. What did people in Europe call America?
   Old World   New World   Small World

Skill Builder

Using Map Directions   The four main directions are **north**, **south**, **east**, and **west**. On maps, these directions are shown by a **compass rose**.

You can also use the letters N, S, E, and W to show directions on a compass rose. Write the letters **N**, **S**, **E**, and **W** on the compass rose in the correct place. One letter is done for you.

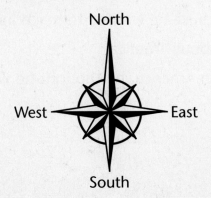

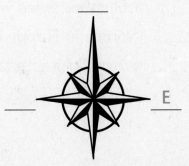

Look back at the map on page 9. Then finish each sentence with the word **north**, **south**, **east**, or **west**.

1. Europe is _____ of the Atlantic Ocean.

2. North America is _____ of the Atlantic Ocean.

3. South America is _____ of North America.

4. Europe is _____ of Africa.

Think and Apply

Finding the Main Idea   A **main idea** is an important idea in the chapter. Less important ideas support the main idea. Read each group of sentences below. One of the three sentences is a main idea. The other two sentences support the main idea. Write an **M** next to the sentence that is the main idea in each group. The first one is done for you.

1. _____ People wanted jewels from India.

   _____ People wanted spices from India.

   __M__ People traveled to India to get jewels and spices.

2. _____ The route to India was dangerous.

   __M__ Columbus wanted to find a better route to India.

   _____ The route to India was very long.

3. _____ In 1492 Columbus sailed for many days to reach America.

   _____ Columbus sailed for 33 days.

   _____ Columbus had three ships—the *Niña*, the *Pinta*, and the *Santa Maria*.

4. _____ Columbus sailed west because he wanted to reach India.

   _____ No one in Europe knew about America.

   _____ When Columbus landed in America, he thought he was in India.

CHAPTER 3
THE SPANISH EXPLORE AMERICA

Estevanico explored the Southwest to find the seven cities of gold for Spain.

Christopher Columbus claimed America for Spain in 1492. People from Spain settled in America. They settled in Mexico and South America. There they heard stories about seven cities that were made of gold. The Spanish wanted to find the seven cities of gold. They began to explore the land north of Mexico. Today this area is the Southwest of the United States.

The Spanish started **slavery** in America. They forced Native Americans to be slaves. In 1503 the Spanish started bringing people from Africa to work as slaves. Each year thousands of Africans became slaves in America. The Spanish forced the slaves to search for gold and silver.

15

Francisco Coronado

Hernando de Soto

The first person to explore the Southwest for Spain was Estevanico. He was an African. In 1539 he searched the Southwest for the seven cities of gold. He never found the seven cities of gold. During his search he was killed by Native Americans.

Francisco Coronado also wanted to find the seven cities of gold. In 1540 Coronado and 300 Spanish soldiers went to the Southwest of the United States. Coronado looked for gold in the Southwest for two years. Coronado found Native American farmers in the Southwest. He found Native American villages made of dried clay. But he never found the seven cities of gold. In 1542 Coronado went home to Mexico. Coronado had explored the Southwest. The king of Spain said that this land belonged to Spain.

Hernando de Soto also wanted to find the seven cities of gold for Spain. De Soto started in Florida with more than 700 people in 1539. While he was looking for gold, he came to a very wide river. It was the Mississippi River. He was the

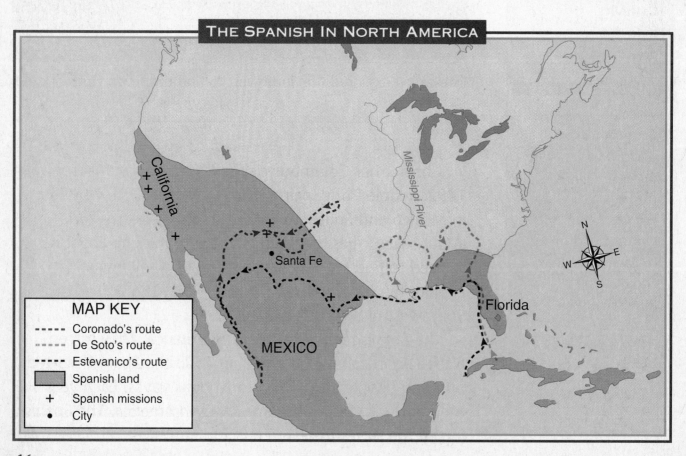

THE SPANISH IN NORTH AMERICA

California

Mississippi River

Santa Fe

Florida

MEXICO

MAP KEY
- - - - Coronado's route
- - - - De Soto's route
- - - - Estevanico's route
Spanish land
+ Spanish missions
• City

The Spanish built many missions in America to teach people how to be Catholics.

first person from Europe to see this river. De Soto never found the seven cities of gold. The Spanish king said that the area De Soto explored belonged to Spain, too.

Many Spanish people came to America to find gold. They did not find gold in the United States. Other Spanish people came to the Southwest of the United States. They came to teach the Native Americans how to be **Catholics**. That is why the Spanish built **missions** in Texas, California, and New Mexico. Every mission had a church. **Priests** worked in the missions. Priests taught the Native Americans to take care of cows, pigs, and sheep. Native Americans also helped the Spanish. They taught the Spanish how to grow tomatoes, potatoes, corn, and beans.

Sometimes Native Americans left the missions because they were not happy. They did not like living with the Spanish. They did not want to follow the Catholic religion. These Native Americans wanted to follow their own religions. Some missions closed when too many Native Americans left.

Other missions became very large. These missions became towns. Santa Fe was one Spanish mission in New Mexico. More and more people came to Santa Fe. Santa Fe became a town. Today Santa Fe is a city. For 300 years the Southwest and Florida belonged to Spain.

★ Read and Remember

Finish the Sentence   Draw a circle around the word or words that finish each sentence.

1. The first person to explore the Southwest for Spain was _____ .
   Estevanico   Columbus   De Soto

2. Coronado explored the _____ of the United States.
   Northwest   Southwest   Southeast

3. De Soto looked for gold in _____ .
   Florida   New Mexico   California

4. De Soto was the first person from Europe to see the _____ .
   Atlantic Ocean   Northeast   Mississippi River

5. Estevanico, Coronado, and De Soto tried to find the _____ cities of gold.
   five   six   seven

6. The Spanish built _____ for the Native Americans.
   farms   stores   missions

Think and Apply ★

Categories   Read the words in each group. Decide how they are alike. Choose the best title in blue print for each group. Write the title on the line above each group. The first one is done for you.

Hernando de Soto   **King of Spain**
Francisco Coronado   **Explorers**

Francisco Coronado

1. looked for seven cities of gold
   explored the Southwest
   found Native American villages

_____

2. said the Southwest belonged to Spain
   said the Southeast belonged to Spain
   ruler of Spain

3. _____

Estevanico
Francisco Coronado
Hernando de Soto

4. _____

looked for seven cities of gold
explored Florida
saw the Mississippi River

Skill Builder

Using a Map Key Maps often show many things. Sometimes maps use little drawings to show what something on the map means. A **map key** tells what those drawings mean. Look at the map key below. On the correct blanks, write what each drawing means.

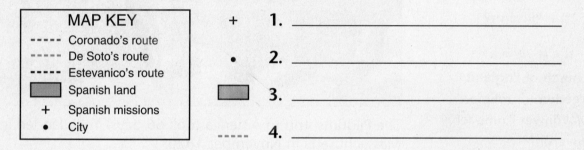

MAP KEY
- - - - - Coronado's route
- - - - - De Soto's route
- - - - - Estevanico's route
▭ Spanish land
+ Spanish missions
• City

+ **1.** _____

• **2.** _____

▭ **3.** _____

- - - - - **4.** _____

Use the map and map key on page 16 to finish these sentences. Circle the number or word that finishes each sentence.

1. There are _____ missions on this map.
20   10   7

2. There were _____ missions in California.
4   7   15

3. The _____ River is on this map.
Mississippi   Florida   Santa Fe

4. De Soto's route began in the _____ .
east   north   west

5. Coronado's route began in the _____ .
north   south   east

CHAPTER 4

THE PILGRIMS' THANKSGIVING

Think About As You Read

1. Why did the Pilgrims want to go to America?
2. What happened to the Pilgrims during their first winter in America?
3. How did Native Americans help the Pilgrims?

NEW WORDS

Church of England
freedom of religion
Mayflower Compact
governor
peace treaty

PEOPLE & PLACES

Pilgrims
England
Holland
Dutch
English
Massachusetts
Plymouth
Massasoit
Squanto

The Pilgrims' trip to America took 66 days. They landed in Massachusetts in November 1620.

A long time ago, the Pilgrims lived in England. All the people in England had to pray in the king's church. This church was called the **Church of England**. The Pilgrims did not like the Church of England. They wanted to pray in their own church.

The Pilgrims left England and went to a small country called Holland. There was **freedom of religion** in Holland. The Pilgrims could pray in their own church in Holland.

The people of Holland are called the Dutch. They speak the Dutch language. The Pilgrims did not like living in Holland. They wanted to keep their English ways. They decided to go to America. In America they could live as they wanted and have freedom of religion.

In 1620 the Pilgrims left Holland for America. They had a ship. Their ship was the *Mayflower*. The trip took 66 days. The weather was rainy and cold. Many Pilgrims became sick during the long, cold trip.

At last the *Mayflower* reached America. It landed in Massachusetts. Before leaving their ship, the Pilgrims made a plan for a government. That plan was the **Mayflower Compact**. The plan said the Pilgrims would work together to make laws. The laws would be fair to all. The Pilgrims would not have a king in America. They would choose a **governor** and rule themselves. The Mayflower Compact was the first government in America that allowed people from Europe to rule themselves.

The Pilgrims landed in November. They started a town called Plymouth. The weather was very cold. It was too cold to grow food. The first winter in Plymouth was terrible. There was little food. Many Pilgrims became sick and died.

The Pilgrims' Journey to America

The *Mayflower*

Squanto taught the Pilgrims how to plant corn.

Native Americans lived in forests near Plymouth. They came and helped the Pilgrims. Their leader was Massasoit. He signed a **peace treaty** with the Pilgrims. The Pilgrims and Native Americans lived together in peace. Squanto was a Native American who taught the Pilgrims how to plant corn. He showed the Pilgrims where to find many fish. He taught the Pilgrims to hunt for deer and turkeys in the forests.

The Pilgrims worked hard in Plymouth. They planted seeds to grow food. They built a church. Then they built houses.

By November 1621 the Pilgrims had a lot of food. They would not be hungry that winter. The Pilgrims were very happy.

The Pilgrims had a Thanksgiving party in November 1621. They invited the Native Americans. The Native Americans brought deer to the party. The Pilgrims brought turkeys. This Thanksgiving party lasted three days. The Pilgrims gave thanks to God for helping them. They said "thank you" to the Native Americans for helping them. This was the Pilgrims' first Thanksgiving in America.

The Pilgrims and the Native Americans had their first Thanksgiving in 1621.

⋆ Read and Remember

Circle the Answer   Draw a circle around the correct answer.

1. Where did the Pilgrims first live?
   Holland   England   America

2. What was the name of the Pilgrims' ship?
   Niña   *Mayflower*   *Pinta*

3. Why did the Pilgrims come to America?
   to become farmers   to have freedom of religion
   to meet Native Americans

4. What town in America did the Pilgrims start?
   Massachusetts   Plymouth   Boston

Think and Apply ⋆

Cause and Effect   A **cause** is something that makes something else happen. What happens is called the **effect**.

   Cause   The doorbell rang
   Effect   so Mr. Ruiz answered the door.

Match each cause on the left with an effect on the right. Write the letter of the effect on the correct blank. The first one is done for you.

Cause

1. The Pilgrims did not want to pray in the Church of England, so ___d___

2. The Pilgrims could not keep their English ways in Holland, so _____

3. The Pilgrims had little food for their first winter, so _____

4. The Native Americans wanted peace, so _____

5. The Pilgrims had a lot of food for their second winter, so _____

Effect

a. many Pilgrims died.

b. Massasoit signed a peace treaty with the Pilgrims.

c. they had a Thanksgiving party to thank God and the Native Americans.

d. they went to Holland.

e. they went to America.

Journal Writing

Write a paragraph in your journal that tells why the Pilgrims gave thanks. Give at least three reasons why they were thankful.

Crossword Puzzle

Each sentence below has a word missing. Choose the missing word for each sentence from the words in blue print. Then write the words in the correct places.

——— ACROSS ———

Holland   laws   Massachusetts   turkey

1. The Mayflower Compact said the _____ would be fair to all.

2. The *Mayflower* landed in _____ .

3. The Pilgrims ate _____ for Thanksgiving.

4. There was freedom of religion in _____ .

——— DOWN ———

Plymouth   Native   fish   Dutch

5. The Pilgrims started a town called _____ .

6. The people in Holland speak the _____ language.

7. _____ Americans brought deer to the Thanksgiving party.

8. The Native Americans helped the Pilgrims hunt and _____ .

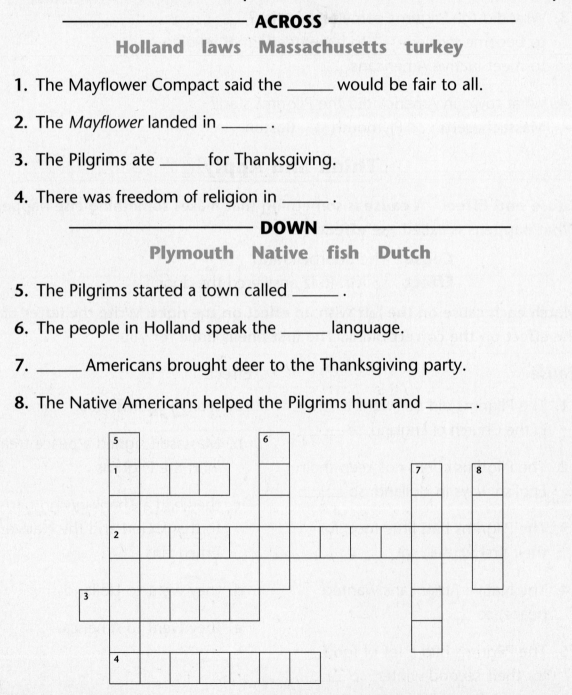

CHAPTER 5

THE ENGLISH SETTLE AMERICA

Think About As You Read

1. Why was the first winter in Jamestown very hard?
2. Which people came to America for freedom of religion?
3. Why did Roger Williams start Rhode Island?

NEW WORDS

colony
settlers
tobacco
religious
in debt

PEOPLE & PLACES

Jamestown
Virginia
Puritans
Roger Williams
Rhode Island
Providence
Anne Hutchinson
Maryland
Quakers
William Penn
Pennsylvania
James Oglethorpe
Georgia

In 1607 the English started Jamestown in Virginia.

The Pilgrims were not the first group of English people to live in America. The first group of English people came to America in 1585, but their **colony** failed.

Before long other English people moved to America. They came for three reasons. Some people came to get rich. Others wanted freedom of religion. Many people came because they thought they could have a better life in America.

In 1607 the English started Jamestown in America. This town was in the Virginia colony. The English came to Jamestown to find gold and become rich. The English did not find gold.

At first the Jamestown **settlers** did not want to grow food or build houses. The settlers were very hungry during the first winter. Many settlers died. More people came to

25

In 1619 the Jamestown settlers brought slaves from Africa to help them grow tobacco.

Jamestown, Virginia

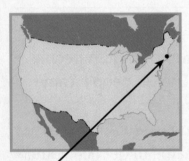

Providence, Rhode Island

live in Jamestown. Then the settlers began to work harder. They built farms and houses.

The settlers began to grow **tobacco** in Jamestown. People would smoke tobacco in pipes. The settlers sold their tobacco to England for a lot of money. Each year the settlers grew more and more tobacco. In 1619 the settlers brought slaves from Africa to help them grow tobacco. After that more Africans were brought to America. Africans were forced to work as slaves in the English colonies.

The Puritans were a group of people who did not want to pray in the Church of England. In 1628 a group of Puritans came to Massachusetts for freedom of religion. Later, more Puritans came. Everyone in Massachusetts had to pray in Puritan churches. The Puritans did not let other people have freedom of religion.

Roger Williams lived with the Puritans. He told them that everyone should have freedom of religion. He left Massachusetts and traveled through the forests. Roger Williams met Native Americans who helped him. He bought land from them. Roger Williams started the Rhode Island colony on that land in 1636. He started the city of Providence in Rhode Island. Providence was the first city in America where there was freedom of religion for all.

Anne Hutchinson was a woman who lived in Massachusetts. Her **religious** ideas were different from the Puritan ideas. Anne Hutchinson left Massachusetts. She went to Rhode Island in 1638 and started a new town.

More English people came to America for freedom of religion. Catholics were sent to jail if they prayed in Catholic churches in England. So 300 Catholics came to America in 1634. They started a colony called Maryland.

The Quakers were another group of people who would not pray in the Church of England. William Penn was a Quaker. In 1681 William Penn started the Pennsylvania colony. He bought the land for his colony from Native Americans. The Native Americans liked William Penn. There was peace in the Pennsylvania colony. Everyone had freedom of religion in Pennsylvania.

In England there were some people who did not have any money. People who were **in debt** were put into jail. These people could not work or help their families. James Oglethorpe started the Georgia colony to help these people. In 1733 James Oglethorpe went to Georgia with 120 of these people. They worked hard in Georgia. They started farms and built homes. Poor people from many countries in Europe came to live and work in the Georgia colony.

Each year more people came to live in the English colonies along the Atlantic Ocean. By 1753 there were 13 English colonies along the Atlantic Ocean.

William Penn

James Oglethorpe

Anne Hutchinson's ideas were different from the ideas of other Puritans.

Read and Remember

Write the Answer   Write a sentence to answer each question.

1. What were three reasons English people came to America? _____

   _____

   _____

2. Why did the English come to Jamestown? _____

   _____

3. Why were African slaves brought to Jamestown? _____

   _____

4. Why did the Puritans come to America? _____

   _____

5. Which was the first city in America to allow freedom of religion for all? _____

   _____

6. Why did the Catholics come to America? _____

   _____

7. Who started the Pennsylvania colony? _____

   _____

8. Who did James Oglethorpe bring to Georgia? _____

   _____

Journal Writing

Which colony would you want to live in if you had moved to America in 1755?
Write a paragraph in your journal that tells which colony you would choose.
Explain your reasons.

Think and Apply

Drawing Conclusions   Read the first two sentences below. Then read the third sentence. Notice how it follows from the first two sentences. It is called a **conclusion**.

> There was no freedom of religion in England.
> The Pilgrims wanted to pray in their own church.

CONCLUSION   The Pilgrims left England to find freedom of religion.

Read the first two sentences. Then look in the box for the conclusion you can make. Write the letter of the conclusion on the blank. The first one is done for you.

1. The Jamestown settlers did not want to grow food.
    They did not build houses.

    Conclusion ___d___

2. The Puritans did not let people have freedom of religion.
    Roger Williams wanted freedom of religion.

    Conclusion _____

3. The Puritans did not let people have freedom of religion.
    Anne Hutchinson's religious ideas were different from the Puritan ideas.

    Conclusion _____

4. There was freedom of religion in Pennsylvania.
    The Native Americans liked William Penn.

    Conclusion _____

5. Many English people were in jail for debt.
    James Oglethorpe wanted to help these people.

    Conclusion _____

> **a.** She left Massachusetts.
> **b.** He started a colony with people from English jails.
> **c.** He left Massachusetts to start his own colony.
> **d.** They were hungry and cold the first winter.
> **e.** The colony was very peaceful.

Skill Builder

Reading a Historical Map   A **historical map** shows how an area used to look. The historical map on this page shows the 13 English colonies in the year 1753.

The 13 colonies are numbered on the map in the order that they were started. Write the name of each colony on the blank line that matches the number of the colony on the map. The first one is done for you.

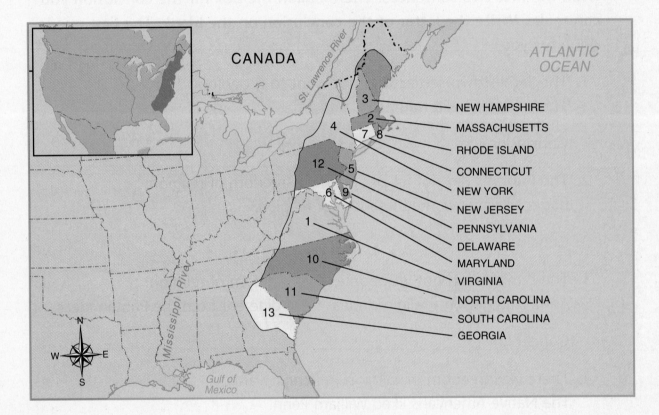

1. _____Virginia_____

2. _____

3. _____

4. _____

5. _____

6. _____

7. _____

8. _____

9. _____

10. _____

11. _____

12. _____

13. _____

CHAPTER 6 THE FRENCH COME TO AMERICA

Think About As You Read

1. Why did the French come to America?
2. How did Native Americans help the French?
3. How did France lose its land in America?

NEW WORDS

short cut
body of water
snowshoes

PEOPLE & PLACES

France
King Louis
Jacques Cartier
Canada
St. Lawrence River
Sieur de la Salle
Gulf of Mexico
Louisiana
St. Louis
New Orleans
George Washington
Virginia
North America

Jacques Cartier explored the St. Lawrence River for France.

Many English people came to America for freedom of religion. Many poor people came to America to earn money. We learned that Spanish people came to America to find gold. People from France also came to America. People from France are called the French.

King Louis of France wanted to find a **short cut** to Asia. In 1534 the king sent Jacques Cartier to America. Cartier wanted to find a river in America that he could follow west all the way to Asia. Cartier sailed to Canada. Cartier could not find a river that went to Asia. He explored the St. Lawrence River. Look at the map on page 33. Find the St. Lawrence River. Cartier said that all the land around the St. Lawrence River belonged to France. French land in America was called New France.

La Salle called the land around the Mississippi River "Louisiana."

Sieur de la Salle

Jacques Cartier

Sieur de la Salle also explored America for France. In 1682 La Salle traveled from the St. Lawrence River to the Mississippi River. Then he paddled a canoe down the Mississippi River to the south. In the south there is a **body of water** called the Gulf of Mexico. La Salle was the first person we know of who traveled all the way down the Mississippi River to the Gulf of Mexico.

La Salle called the land near the Mississippi River "Louisiana." He put a big cross and a French flag on the land of Louisiana. La Salle said, "All the land around the Mississippi River belongs to King Louis of France. I am calling this land 'Louisiana'." The land around the Mississippi River and the land around the St. Lawrence River were part of New France.

The French king sent more people to America. The French started two cities on the Mississippi River. These two French cities were St. Louis and New Orleans. New Orleans was near the Gulf of Mexico.

The French owned much more land in America than the English. But not many French people wanted to move to America. They did not build many farms and towns in America. The French did not allow freedom of religion. Only Catholics were allowed to live in New France. The French colony grew very slowly.

There were some French people who wanted to move to America. They came for two reasons. One reason was to find furs. Native Americans hunted many animals for their furs. The French traded with Native Americans for these furs. In France they sold these furs for a lot of money. The second reason the French came was to teach Native Americans how to be Catholics. French priests taught their religion to Native Americans.

Native Americans helped the French in many ways. They taught the French how to trap animals for furs. They taught the French how to use canoes to travel on rivers. They also showed the French how to make **snowshoes**. Many parts of New France had lots of snow in the winter. When they wore snowshoes, the French could walk on very deep snow.

Native Americans had fewer fights with the French than with the Spanish or the English. The Spanish had forced Native Americans to work as slaves. The French never treated them as slaves. The English took land away from the Native

French fur trapper wearing snowshoes

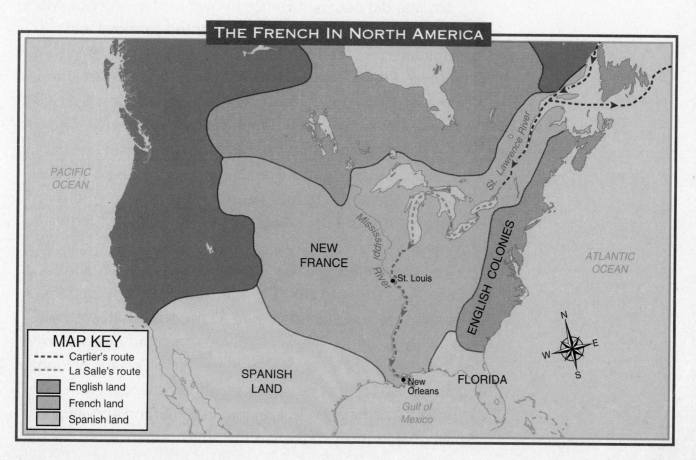

THE FRENCH IN NORTH AMERICA

PACIFIC OCEAN

NEW FRANCE

Mississippi River

St. Louis

St. Lawrence River

ENGLISH COLONIES

ATLANTIC OCEAN

SPANISH LAND

New Orleans

FLORIDA

Gulf of Mexico

MAP KEY
- - - - Cartier's route
- - - - La Salle's route
English land
French land
Spanish land

N E W S

In 1763 France lost most of its land to England in the French and Indian War.

Americans in order to build farms and towns. The French did not take Native American lands.

England did not want France to own land in America. Many English people in the 13 colonies wanted to move west to Louisiana. France did not want English people to live in Louisiana. England and France had been enemies in Europe for many years. They became enemies in America. By 1754 England and France were fighting a war in America. This war was called the French and Indian War. Some Native Americans fought for the French, and some fought for the English. George Washington lived in the Virginia colony. He helped the English soldiers fight. The soldiers fought for many years.

The war ended in 1763. France lost the French and Indian War. England won the war. After the war, England owned Canada. England owned all the land that was east of the Mississippi River. Spain owned the land that was west of the Mississippi River. St. Louis and New Orleans belonged to Spain. France lost most of its land in America. France kept two small islands in Canada. In 1763 England and Spain owned most of the land in North America.

★ Read and Remember

Finish the Story Use the words in blue print to finish the story. Write the words you choose on the correct blanks.

furs   Louisiana   Mississippi   canoes   Catholic   French

The French explorer La Salle traveled down the _____

River. He paddled all the way to the Gulf of Mexico. La Salle called all the land

around the Mississippi River "_____." This land became part of

the large French colony called New France. Some French people came to America

to find _____ . Others came to teach the _____

religion to Native Americans. Native Americans taught the French how to use

_____ and snowshoes. In 1763 the _____ lost

the French and Indian War to England.

Think and Apply ★

Fact or Opinion   A **fact** is a true statement. An **opinion** is a statement that tells what a person thinks.

> **Fact**   The French explored America.
> **Opinion**   The French were the best explorers.

Write **F** next to each fact below. Write **O** next to each opinion. You should find three sentences that are opinions.

_____ 1. The French king wanted to find a shortcut to Asia.

_____ 2. Jacques Cartier explored the St. Lawrence River.

_____ 3. La Salle was a smarter explorer than Cartier.

_____ 4. Before 1754 France owned more land in America than England.

_____ 5. New France was a better place to live than the English colonies.

_____ 6. The French were stronger soldiers than the English.

Skill Builder

Using Map Directions   In Chapter 2 you learned that there are four main directions on a map. They are north, south, east, and west. A compass rose also shows four in-between directions. They are **northeast**, **southeast**, **northwest**, and **southwest**. Southeast is between south and east. Southwest is between south and west. Sometimes the in-between directions are shortened to **NE**, **SE**, **NW**, and **SW**.

Write the shortened in-between directions on the compass rose below. One in-between direction is done for you.

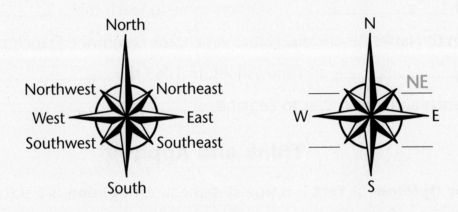

Look at the map on page 37. Then circle the word that finishes each sentence.

1. The St. Lawrence River is in the _____ .
   northeast   northwest   southwest

2. The English colonies were in the _____ .
   northwest   southwest   east

3. The Mississippi River was _____ of the English colonies.
   south   west   east

4. Florida is in the _____ .
   southeast   northeast   northwest

5. The Atlantic Ocean was to the _____ of the English colonies.
   north   south   east

6. New Orleans is in the _____ .
   northwest   northeast   south

The historical map on this page shows the Spanish, French, and English colonies in North America in 1754. Study the map. Then use the words in blue print to finish the story.

Atlantic Ocean   Gulf of Mexico   New Orleans   Florida
Southwest   St. Lawrence   Jamestown

Spain had land in the Southeast called _____ . Spain also had land in the _____ . Then in 1607 the English started _____ in the Virginia colony. All of the 13 English colonies were near the _____ .

In 1534 Cartier explored a river in Canada called the _____ River. La Salle traveled south on the Mississippi River to the _____ . The French built the city of _____ near the Gulf of Mexico.

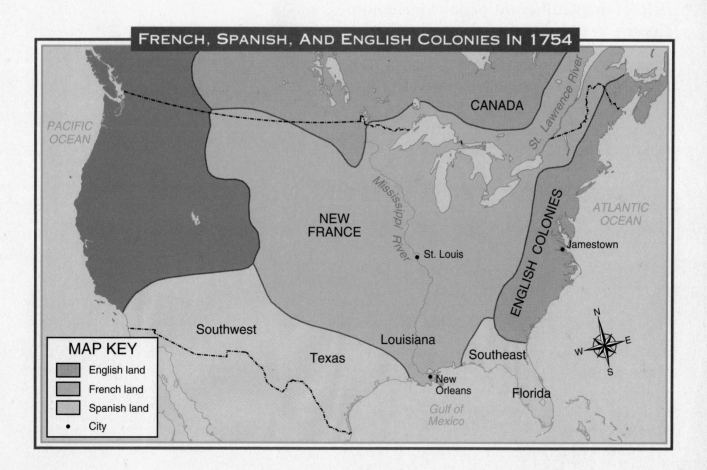

FRENCH, SPANISH, AND ENGLISH COLONIES IN 1754

PACIFIC OCEAN

CANADA

St. Lawrence River

NEW FRANCE

Mississippi River

St. Louis

ENGLISH COLONIES

ATLANTIC OCEAN

Jamestown

Southwest

Louisiana

Texas

Southeast

New Orleans

Florida

Gulf of Mexico

N E S W

MAP KEY
- English land
- French land
- Spanish land
- • City

UNIT 2

BUILDING A NEW NATION

Imagine what it was like to live in America in 1776. Many Americans were angry at the British leaders who ruled over them. They were angry at unfair laws that the British leaders wrote for the colonies. Americans became so angry at these laws that they decided to fight.

Americans in the 13 colonies were not ready to fight. They did not have enough guns, money, or soldiers to fight for their freedom. The British army was much stronger. How could the Americans win? It would take the help of many different people, including George Washington.

What would you have done if you had lived in 1776? Would you have joined the fight to make the United States of America a free country? As you read Unit 2, think about how Americans built a new country.

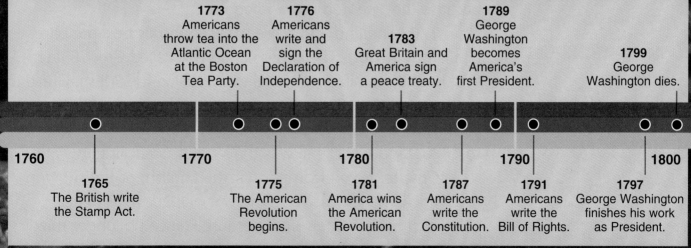

1773
Americans throw tea into the Atlantic Ocean at the Boston Tea Party.

1776
Americans write and sign the Declaration of Independence.

1783
Great Britain and America sign a peace treaty.

1789
George Washington becomes America's first President.

1799
George Washington dies.

1760

1770

1780

1790

1800

1765
The British write the Stamp Act.

1775
The American Revolution begins.

1781
America wins the American Revolution.

1787
Americans write the Constitution.

1791
Americans write the Bill of Rights.

1797
George Washington finishes his work as President.

7 AMERICANS FIGHT FOR FREEDOM

CHAPTER

Think About As You Read

1. Why did Americans think that the new laws from Great Britain were unfair?
2. What happened during the Boston Tea Party?
3. Why did Americans start to fight against Great Britain in 1775?

NEW WORDS

nation
tax
Stamp Act
Parliament
port
Boston Tea Party
American Revolution

PEOPLE & PLACES

Americans
Great Britain
British
King George III
Boston

British leaders made laws in a large building called Parliament.

Many people from England came to live in America. They came to live in the 13 colonies. The people who lived in the colonies were called Americans. Many people came to America because they wanted more freedom.

In 1707 England and three small countries became part of a larger **nation**. The larger nation was called Great Britain. People who lived in Great Britain were called the British. Great Britain ruled the 13 American colonies. The king of Great Britain was the king of the American colonies. From 1760 to 1820, King George III was the king of Great Britain.

In Chapter 6 you learned that the English, or British, won the French and Indian War. The war helped the American colonies. Americans felt safer because France no longer ruled Canada. Great Britain ruled Canada after this war. The British had spent a lot of money to fight the French. Great Britain paid for soldiers, guns, and food for its army. The British wanted the colonies to help pay for the French and Indian War.

The British made new laws. The laws said that Americans had to send some of their money to Great Britain. The money that Americans had to send was called **tax** money. This tax money would help Great Britain get back the money it had spent on the war.

In 1765 the British made a new tax law called the **Stamp Act**. The Stamp Act said that Americans had to pay a tax on things like newspapers. A special stamp was placed on the newspaper to show that the tax was paid.

Americans did not like the new tax law. Some Americans decided not to pay the new taxes. Some Americans burned stamps to show that they did not like the new law. They said the new law was not fair. It was not fair because Americans did not help write the tax law.

In Great Britain the British helped make their own laws. They did this by voting for leaders who would make laws for them. These British leaders met in a large building called **Parliament**. In Parliament the leaders wrote laws for Great Britain. Americans wanted to send their own leaders to help write laws in Parliament. The British would not let Americans write laws in Parliament.

King George III

Parliament Building

Americans burned stamps to show they did not like the Stamp Act.

The Parliament made more tax laws for the colonies. The British leaders did not let Americans help write any of these laws. Americans did not like the new laws that the British wrote for them.

In 1773 the British made another law. This law said that Americans must pay a tea tax. This meant that Americans had to pay a tax when they paid for their tea. Americans had to send the tax money to Great Britain. Americans were very angry because they did not help write the tea tax law.

Boston was a large **port** city in Massachusetts near the Atlantic Ocean. Three ships with boxes of tea came to Boston. The Americans did not want to pay a tea tax. They did not want the tea. They wanted to send the tea ships back to Great Britain. The British said that Americans had to pay for the tea.

Some Americans decided to throw the boxes of tea into the ocean. One night in 1773, they put on Native American clothes. They went on the tea ships. The Americans threw every box of tea into the Atlantic Ocean. This is known as the **Boston Tea Party**. The Boston Tea Party made King George very angry.

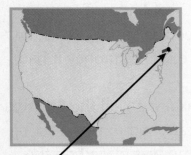

Boston, Massachusetts

At the Boston Tea Party, Americans threw British tea into the ocean.

The first battle of the American Revolution was in Massachusetts.

King George punished the people of Boston. He closed Boston's port. Ships could not come to or go from the port. He said the port would be closed until Americans paid for all the tea. He sent many British soldiers to Massachusetts.

The British had made another law that Americans did not like. This law said that Americans must give the British soldiers food and a place to sleep. The soldiers paid when they ate and slept in Americans' homes. But Americans did not like the British soldiers. They did not want the soldiers in their homes. And now King George sent more soldiers to Massachusetts. Americans were becoming angrier and angrier.

The angry Americans formed an army. In 1775 American soldiers began to fight Great Britain for freedom. The fighting began in Massachusetts. The British won the first battles. But the Americans would not stop fighting. Americans were fighting for the same freedom that people had in Great Britain. They wanted the freedom to write their own laws. A war had started in 1775 between Great Britain and America. Americans called this war the **American Revolution**.

★ Read and Remember

Match Up   Finish each sentence in Group A with words from Group B. Write the letter of the correct answer on the blank line. The first one is done for you.

Group A

1. Great Britain wanted the colonies to help pay for the ___c___

2. The new tax laws were not fair to Americans because _____

3. During the Boston Tea Party, the Americans went on three British ships and _____

4. After the Boston Tea Party, King George punished Americans by _____

5. In 1775 Americans began fighting a war with Great Britain that the Americans _____

Group B

a. closing the port of Boston.

b. called the American Revolution.

c. French and Indian War.

d. threw all the tea into the ocean.

e. Americans did not help write laws in Parliament.

Think and Apply ★

Understanding Different Points of View   People can look in different ways at something that happens. Look at these two points of view about a math test.

The math test was very hard.
The math test was fair.

In 1775 the Americans and the British had different points of view about how to rule the 13 colonies. Read each pair of sentences below. Write **American** next to the sentences that show the American point of view. Write **British** next to the sentences that show the British point of view. The first sentence is done for you.

____British____   1. Only people in Great Britain should write laws in Parliament.

_____   2. Americans should help write their laws in Parliament.

_____ **3.** Americans should not pay a tea tax if they did not help write the tax law.

_____ **4.** Americans should pay for all the tea they threw in the ocean.

_____ **5.** Americans have enough freedom.

_____ **6.** Americans should fight the British for more freedom.

 **Skill Builder**

Reading a Time Line   A **time line** is a drawing that shows years on a line. **Look at this time line. Read the time line from left to right.**

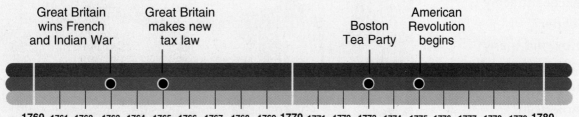

Great Britain wins French and Indian War

Great Britain makes new tax law

Boston Tea Party

American Revolution begins

1760 1761 1762 1763 1764 1765 1766 1767 1768 1769 1770 1771 1772 1773 1774 1775 1776 1777 1778 1779 1780

The year 1765 comes before 1766, and 1767 comes after 1766.

  1. What year comes after 1774? _____

  2. What year comes before 1775? _____

Events are sometimes placed on time lines. Read the events on the time line. **Then answer each question.**

  3. When did Great Britain win the French and Indian War? _____

  4. When did Great Britain make a new tax law? _____

  5. When was the Boston Tea Party? _____

 **Journal Writing**

What would you do if you were an American living in the 13 colonies in 1775? Would you help the Americans or King George? Write a paragraph in your journal that tells what you would do and why.

A NEW COUNTRY IS BORN

CHAPTER 8

Think About As You Read

1. Why did Americans write the Declaration of Independence?
2. Why was George Washington an excellent army leader?
3. How did many different people help win the American Revolution?

NEW WORDS

independent
Declaration of Independence
equal
Loyalists
General

PEOPLE & PLACES

Thomas Jefferson
Philadelphia
Friedrich von Steuben
Germany
Thaddeus Kosciusko
Poland
African Americans
James Armistead
Molly Pitcher
Haym Salomon
Jewish American

In 1776 Thomas Jefferson and other leaders wrote the Declaration of Independence.

The American Revolution began in the year 1775. At first Americans were fighting the British because they wanted more freedom. American leaders wrote to King George. They asked him to let Americans write their own laws in Parliament. But King George would not give Americans more freedom. So in 1776 many Americans decided that they wanted the colonies to become **independent**. Independent means "to be free."

Americans decided to tell the world that the colonies no longer belonged to Great Britain. In 1776 Thomas Jefferson and a few other leaders were asked to write the **Declaration of Independence**. The Declaration of Independence was an important paper. It said, "All men are created **equal**."

This means that all people are just as important as a king. It also said all people should have freedom. The Declaration of Independence also said that the 13 colonies were an independent nation.

The leaders of the 13 colonies went to Philadelphia in the Pennsylvania colony. On July 4, 1776, the leaders signed the Declaration of Independence in Philadelphia.

Some Americans in the colonies did not want the colonies to be free. These people were called **Loyalists**. They fought for Great Britain during the American Revolution.

The American Revolution lasted six years. During that time George Washington was the leader of the American army. The soldiers called him **General** Washington. George Washington was a good leader. He tried to be fair to the soldiers, and he was a good fighter. The Americans lost many battles, or fights. They were often hungry and cold during the winters. But General Washington did not give up. The Americans continued to fight for independence.

Many people tried to help the Americans win the war. France sent French soldiers to America. French soldiers helped the Americans fight against the British.

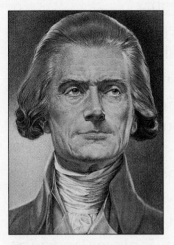

Thomas Jefferson

The Declaration of Independence

General Washington was the leader of the American army. He is shown here with his soldiers during the cold winter.

James Armistead

Deborah Sampson

People from other nations also helped Americans fight. Friedrich von Steuben came from Germany to help. He taught Americans how to be better soldiers. Thaddeus Kosciusko came from Poland to help Americans fight.

All kinds of Americans fought together in the war. Farmers, sailors, business owners, and teachers all became soldiers.

About five thousand African Americans fought against the British. They fought in every important battle. James Armistead was a brave African American soldier. He was a spy for the Americans.

Women also helped win the war. They did the farm work when the men were fighting. They grew food for the soldiers. They made clothes for the army. Women also cared for soldiers who were hurt during the war. Deborah Sampson and a few other women dressed like soldiers and fought in the war.

One woman, Molly Pitcher, brought water to American soldiers when they were fighting. Molly's husband, John, was a soldier. One day John was hurt during a battle. He could not fight. Molly took John's place in the battle against the British soldiers.

Molly Pitcher fought in the American Revolution.

Americans cheered for Washington and his soldiers when they won the American Revolution.

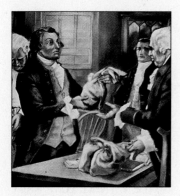

Haym Salomon

Haym Salomon was a Jewish American who helped the Americans win. He had left Poland to come to America for freedom of religion. Haym Salomon worked hard and became rich. He knew the American army had little money. The soldiers did not have enough food, clothes, or guns. Some soldiers did not even have shoes. Haym Salomon gave most of his money to the American army. The soldiers bought food, guns, shoes, and clothes with this money. Haym Salomon was a poor man when he died. He had given most of his money to help the Americans win.

The American Revolution ended in 1781. The Americans had won. Great Britain and the colonies signed a peace treaty in 1783. People in other countries learned how the Americans won their fight for freedom. Soon people in other countries would want more freedom, too.

Great Britain lost the American Revolution. When the war was over, the 13 colonies were independent. Now the 13 colonies were called 13 states. The Americans called their new country the United States of America.

Read and Remember

Finish the Sentence Draw a circle around the date, word, or words that finish each sentence.

1. Americans in the 13 colonies told the world they were independent in _____ .
   1765   1776   1783

2. The Declaration of Independence said, "All men are created _____ ."
   smart   slow   equal

3. Americans signed the Declaration of Independence in _____ .
   Boston   Philadelphia   Jamestown

4. Many _____ soldiers helped the Americans fight.
   French   British   Russians

5. _____ taught Americans how to be better soldiers.
   King George   Friedrich von Steuben   Molly Pitcher

6. _____ was a brave African American soldier.
   Haym Salomon   James Armistead   Thomas Jefferson

7. The American Revolution ended in _____ .
   1765   1776   1781

True or False Write **T** next to each sentence that is true. Write **F** next to each sentence that is false.

_____ 1. The 13 colonies became independent in the French and Indian War.

_____ 2. Thomas Jefferson helped write the Declaration of Independence.

_____ 3. Some Americans who fought for Great Britain during the American Revolution were called Loyalists.

_____ 4. France sent French soldiers to help Americans fight.

_____ 5. Americans called their new country the United Colonies of America.

Think and Apply

Drawing Conclusions   Read each pair of sentences. Then look in the box for the conclusion you can make. Write the letter of the conclusion on the blank.

_____ 1. Americans in the 13 colonies decided to become independent.
Americans wanted to tell the world that they were independent.

_____ 2. Americans called Loyalists fought for Great Britain during the American Revolution.
The Loyalists liked King George.

_____ 3. George Washington was fair to the soldiers.
George Washington lost many battles but never gave up.

_____ 4. Many women made food and clothes for the army.
Women took care of soldiers who were hurt.

_____ 5. Haym Salomon was a rich man.
He knew the American army needed a lot of money.

Conclusions

  a. Americans asked Thomas Jefferson to write the Declaration of Independence.

  b. George Washington was an excellent army leader.

  c. Haym Salomon gave most of his money to the American army.

  d. Some Americans did not want the colonies to become independent.

  e. American women helped in many ways during the war.

Journal Writing

Imagine that you were a news reporter in 1776. Write a short news story about the signing of the Declaration of Independence. Tell why Americans wrote the Declaration, and write some of the things it said.

CHAPTER 9

THE CONSTITUTION

Many leaders helped write the United States Constitution.

Think About As You Read

1. Why did the United States need a constitution after the American Revolution?
2. How do Americans write their own laws?
3. How does the Bill of Rights protect your freedom?

NEW WORDS

constitution
Congress
Senate
House of Representatives
senators
representatives
Supreme Court
judges
capital
freedom of the press
amendments
Bill of Rights

PEOPLE & PLACES

Capitol
White House
Washington, D.C.

The American Revolution was won in 1781. The United States was now an independent country with 13 states. The new country needed new laws. A **constitution** is a group of laws. The leaders of the United States decided to write laws, or a constitution, for their new country. In 1787 leaders from 12 of the states went to Philadelphia. In Philadelphia the leaders wrote the United States Constitution.

Before the American Revolution, Great Britain made laws for the American colonies. Americans liked the way the British voted for leaders to write laws in Parliament. A group of men planned the Constitution so that Americans could help write their own laws. How do Americans do this?

The United States
Constitution

The Constitution says that Americans should choose, or vote for, people to work for them in their government. Our country's laws are made by men and women in **Congress**. In some ways our Congress is like Great Britain's Parliament. Americans vote for people who will make laws for them in Congress. There are two houses, or parts, of Congress. The **Senate** and the **House of Representatives** are the two houses of Congress.

Men and women who write laws are called **senators** and **representatives**. Every state sends two senators to work in the Senate. States with many people send many representatives to work in the House of Representatives. States with fewer people send fewer representatives to work in the House of Representatives. The senators and representatives meet in a building called the Capitol. The Constitution says that Americans should vote for people to be their senators and representatives. Americans help write their own laws by voting for their senators and representatives.

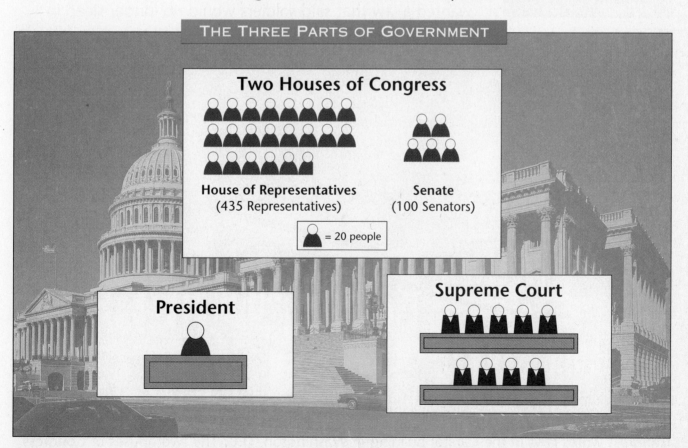

THE THREE PARTS OF GOVERNMENT

Two Houses of Congress

House of Representatives
(435 Representatives)

Senate
(100 Senators)

= 20 people

President

Supreme Court

Congress, the President, and the Supreme Court work together to make laws.

Bill of Rights

The White House

Americans vote for a President every four years. The President carries out the country's laws. The President helps make our laws. The White House is where the President lives and works.

The Constitution also gives the United States its **Supreme Court**. Nine **judges** work in the Supreme Court. In the Supreme Court, judges decide whether or not our laws agree with the Constitution.

The White House, the Capitol, and the Supreme Court buildings are in the city of Washington, D.C. It is the **capital** of our country.

Some of our leaders were not happy with the Constitution when it was written in 1787. The Constitution did not say that Americans had freedom of religion. The Constitution did not say that Americans had **freedom of the press**. "Freedom of the press" means the government cannot tell people what they can say in newspapers and books. British soldiers had often stayed in American homes. Americans wanted a law that said soldiers would no longer sleep in American homes.

Congress writes laws in the Capitol building in Washington, D.C. The two houses of Congress are the Senate and the House of Representatives.

The President sometimes meets with all the senators and representatives of Congress in the Capitol building.

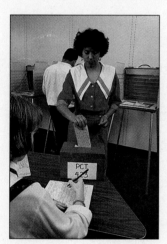

American voting

In 1791 our leaders added ten **amendments**, or new laws, to the Constitution. These ten amendments are called the **Bill of Rights**. The Bill of Rights is now part of our Constitution. What are some of these rights? Every American has freedom of religion. Every American has freedom of the press. Americans do not have to let soldiers sleep in their homes. The Bill of Rights gives every American many freedoms.

Since 1791, seventeen more amendments have been added to the Constitution. Our Constitution now has 27 amendments. These amendments were added because our leaders wanted laws to be fair to all Americans. As our country changes, more amendments may be added to the Constitution.

Today our Constitution is more than 200 years old. The leaders of 1787 gave us good laws. These laws helped America become a great country.

Read and Remember

Write the Answer   Write one or more sentences to answer each question.

1. Where did Americans write the Constitution? _____

_____

2. What does the President do? _____

_____

3. What do senators and representatives do in Congress? _____

_____

4. How many senators does each state have in the United States Senate? _____

_____

5. In what city are the White House, Capitol, and Supreme Court buildings?

_____

6. Why did the leaders add the Bill of Rights to the Constitution? _____

_____

7. What are some of the rights that the Bill of Rights added to the Constitution?

_____

_____

Think and Apply

Finding the Main Idea   Read each group of sentences below. One of the sentences is a main idea. Two sentences support the main idea. Write an **M** next to the sentence that is the main idea in each group.

1. _____   Americans were angry when the British wrote laws for them.

   _____   Americans made a constitution that said they could write their own laws.

   _____   Americans wanted to make their own laws.

2. _____ The Constitution says Americans can choose people to work in their government.

_____ Americans vote for their senators and representatives.

_____ Americans vote for their President every four years.

3. _____ The Constitution did not say that Americans had freedom of the press.

_____ In 1791 America's leaders added the Bill of Rights to the Constitution.

_____ The Constitution did not say that Americans had freedom of religion.

4. _____ The President and the Supreme Court are two parts of the government.

_____ The Senate and the House of Representatives make up one part of the government.

_____ The United States government has three parts.

5. _____ Americans wrote the Constitution in 1787.

_____ The Constitution has helped our country for more than 200 years.

_____ Americans have added 27 amendments to the Constitution.

Skill Builder

Reading a Diagram A diagram is a picture that helps you understand something. The diagram on page 53 helps you understand our government. Look back at the diagram. Then finish each sentence with a word in blue print.

President   senators   nine   three   435

1. The United States government has _____ parts.

2. The government has one _____ .

3. The government has _____ Supreme Court judges.

4. There are fewer _____ than representatives.

5. There are _____ members of the House of Representatives.

Think About As You Read

1. What kinds of work did Benjamin Franklin do in Boston and Philadelphia?
2. How did Benjamin Franklin help the city of Philadelphia?
3. How did Benjamin Franklin help the American colonies become independent?

NEW WORDS

printing shop
printer
published
electric sparks

PEOPLE & PLACES

Benjamin Franklin

When Ben was a young man, he worked in his brother's printing shop.

Benjamin Franklin was born in Boston in 1706. He had 16 brothers and sisters. In those days, people used candles to light their homes. Ben's father earned money by making soap and candles.

Ben was a smart boy. He loved to read books. Ben went to school until he was ten years old. Then Ben made soap and candles with his father.

Ben had an older brother named James. James owned a **printing shop**. When Ben was 12 years old, he went to work for James. Ben became a **printer**. Ben and James **published** a newspaper together. Ben enjoyed his work, but he did not like working with James. Ben decided to run away from Boston.

Ben ran away. He went to Philadelphia. Ben worked in a printing shop in Philadelphia. When Ben was 24 years old, he published his own newspaper. People read Ben's newspaper in all 13 American colonies.

Ben wanted Philadelphia to be a better city. Ben started the city's first hospital. He started a fire department. He started a school in Philadelphia. Ben started Philadelphia's first public library.

Ben knew there was something called electricity. He wanted to learn more about electricity. One night there were rain and lightning outside. Ben tied a key to the end of a kite string. He flew the kite outside. Lightning hit the kite. **Electric sparks** jumped off the key. Then Ben knew that lightning is a kind of electricity. People all over America and Europe read about Ben's work with electricity. Ben became famous.

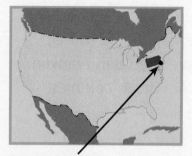

Philadelphia, Pennsylvania

Ben used a kite and a key to show that lightning is a kind of electricity.

Benjamin Franklin

Ben wanted the American colonies to become an independent country. He helped Thomas Jefferson write the Declaration of Independence in 1776. Ben was one of the men who signed the Declaration. Ben wanted to help his country win the American Revolution. He was then seventy years old. He was too old to be a soldier. Ben went to France. He asked the French people to help the Americans fight. The French people liked Ben Franklin. France sent soldiers and ships to the American colonies. France helped the Americans win the war.

In 1787 Ben was 81 years old. He had another job to do. He helped write the Constitution. Ben and the other leaders spent four months writing the Constitution in Philadelphia.

Benjamin Franklin died in Philadelphia when he was 84 years old. He was a very famous American. He helped Philadelphia become a great city, and he helped the United States become a free country.

Ben went to France to get help for the American soldiers.

★ Read and Remember

Find the Answers Put a check (✓) next to each sentence below that tells how Ben helped Philadelphia and America. You should check four sentences.

_____ **1.** Ben started a hospital and a public library.

_____ **2.** Ben started a police department.

_____ **3.** Ben started a fire department.

_____ **4.** Ben helped Thomas Jefferson write the Declaration of Independence.

_____ **5.** Ben was a soldier in the American Revolution.

_____ **6.** Ben helped Great Britain during the American Revolution.

_____ **7.** Ben helped write the Constitution in 1787.

Think and Apply ★

Cause and Effect Match each cause on the left with an effect on the right. Write the letter of the effect on the correct blank.

Cause

1. James and Ben did not get along well, so _____

2. Ben learned how to be a printer in Boston, so _____

3. Lightning hit Ben's kite and sparks flew off the key, so _____

4. Ben wanted the American colonies to become independent, so _____

5. Ben knew that America needed help during the American Revolution, so _____

Effect

a. he signed the Declaration of Independence.

b. he went to France to ask for help.

c. Ben learned that lightning is a kind of electricity.

d. Ben ran away to Philadelphia.

e. he found a job as a printer in Philadelphia.

Skill Builder

Reading a Bar Graph **Graphs** are drawings that help you compare facts. The graph on this page is a **bar graph**. It uses bars of different lengths to show facts. The bar graph below shows the **population** of America's three largest cities in 1776. Population means the number of people.

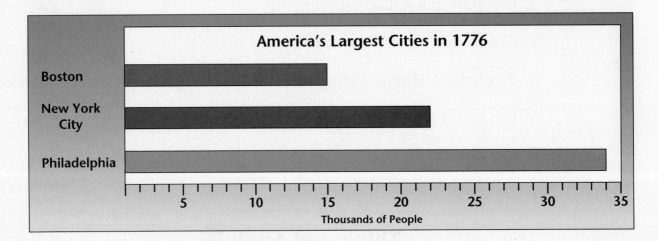

America's Largest Cities in 1776

Boston

New York City

Philadelphia

5   10   15   20   25   30   35

Thousands of People

Use the bar graph to answer each question. Draw a circle around the correct answer.

1. How many people lived in Boston?
   15,000   22,000   34,000

2. How many people lived in Philadelphia?
   15,000   22,000   34,000

3. What was the population of New York City in 1776?
   5,000   10,000   22,000

4. Which city had the largest population in 1776?
   Boston   New York City   Philadelphia

5. Which of these three cities had the smallest population in 1776?
   Boston   New York City   Philadelphia

Journal Writing

Write a paragraph telling why you think Benjamin Franklin was so important in American history.

Think About As You Read

1. How did George Washington help win the American Revolution?
2. How did George Washington help his country after the American Revolution?
3. How did Martha Washington help her country?

NEW WORDS

manage
commander in chief
surrendered
First Lady
boundaries

PEOPLE & PLACES

Martha Washington
Mount Vernon
New York City
Trenton, New Jersey
Yorktown
Pierre L'Enfant
Benjamin Banneker

Many Americans call George Washington the "Father of our Country."

George Washington was born in the Virginia colony on February 22, 1732. George's parents owned a large house with a lot of farm land. George was a quiet, shy boy. His father died when George was 11 years old. George then helped his mother **manage** the family farm. He learned how to be a good farmer.

George was a soldier in Virginia. Do you remember that Great Britain and France were fighting for land in America in 1754? This fight was called the French and Indian War. George became a leader of the Virginia army. He was 22 years old. George and the Americans helped the British win the war.

63

In 1759 George married a wealthy woman named Martha. George and Martha Washington lived in a large, beautiful house in Virginia. They called their home Mount Vernon. There were large farms at Mount Vernon. George loved managing his farms.

In 1775 the American Revolution began. George wanted the American colonies to become independent. He became the **commander in chief** of the American army. This means that he was the leader of all the American soldiers. The soldiers called him General Washington.

George lost a battle in New York City. But he did not give up. He took his army south to Pennsylvania. On Christmas 1776 George took his army to Trenton, New Jersey. Find Trenton on the map on page 65. George knew that the British army would be having Christmas parties. They would not be ready to fight. So George and the Americans surprised the British army. The British army **surrendered**. General Washington won the Battle of Trenton, but the war was not over.

The British and the Americans continued to fight. The American army did not have enough food, clothes, or guns. Many soldiers became sick during the cold winters. Most soldiers liked George Washington. They stayed with him and helped him fight for American freedom.

Martha Washington

Mount Vernon was George and Martha's home in Virginia.

Martha Washington helped the American army during the war. Martha stayed with George during the six cold winters of the American Revolution. She sewed clothes for the soldiers. She fixed their torn shirts and pants. Martha took care of soldiers who became sick or hurt. During the summer Martha managed the home and farms at Mount Vernon.

In 1781 the Americans won an important battle at Yorktown, Virginia. The British army surrendered to George Washington at Yorktown. The American Revolution was over. In 1783 Great Britain and the colonies signed a peace treaty. Then General Washington said good-bye to the army. He was happy to go home to Mount Vernon.

Soon the American people needed George Washington again. They wanted him to help write the Constitution. George helped write the Constitution in Philadelphia in 1787. He wanted to return to Mount Vernon. But the United States needed a President. Americans voted for George Washington.

George Washington became our first President in 1789. Martha Washington became the **First Lady**. The government of the United States was in New York City. So George and

Important battles of the American Revolution

In 1781 British soldiers surrendered to General Washington in Yorktown, Virginia.

In 1789 George Washington became the first President of the United States.

Benjamin Banneker

Martha left Mount Vernon. They traveled to New York City. George was America's hero. As he traveled, crowds everywhere cheered for him.

George wanted the United States to have a new capital city. George found a beautiful place for the capital between Maryland and Virginia. George asked a Frenchman named Pierre L'Enfant to plan the new city.

Benjamin Banneker, a free African American, helped L'Enfant plan the new city. Banneker knew a lot about math and science. He used math and science to help plan the **boundaries** of the new capital. Banneker also wrote to American leaders about ending slavery in the new country. In 1800 the government moved to the new capital. The capital is now called Washington, D.C.

George Washington was President for eight years. As President, George helped the United States become a stronger nation. In 1797 George returned to Mount Vernon. He died at his home in 1799.

George Washington was one of our greatest American leaders. He led our country in war and in peace. Many people call him the "Father of our Country."

★ Read and Remember

Finish the Sentence   Draw a circle around the word or words that finish each sentence.

1. After his father died, George Washington helped his mother _____ the family farm.
   sell   manage   buy

2. George led the Virginia army in the _____ War.
   Revolutionary   Civil   French and Indian

3. George was the _____ of the American army.
   President   commander in chief   captain

4. George lost a battle in _____ .
   Boston   Philadelphia   New York City

5. George won a Christmas battle in _____ .
   New York City   Yorktown   Trenton

6. In 1787 George helped write the _____ .
   Constitution   Bill of Rights   Declaration of Independence

7. When George Washington was President, Martha Washington was _____ .
   Senator   First Lady   Judge

8. Pierre L'Enfant and _____ planned the capital city of Washington, D.C.
   Ben Franklin   James Armistead   Benjamin Banneker

Think and Apply ★

Sequencing Events   Write the numbers **1**, **2**, **3**, **4**, and **5** next to these sentences to show the correct order.

_____ George Washington became the first President of the United States.

_____ George was a leader of the Virginia army in the French and Indian War.

_____ George won the Battle of Trenton on Christmas in 1776.

_____ George helped write the Constitution.

_____ George became the commander in chief of the American army.

Skill Builder

Understanding Decades on a Time Line Sometimes time lines show decades. A **decade** is ten years. Look at this time line.

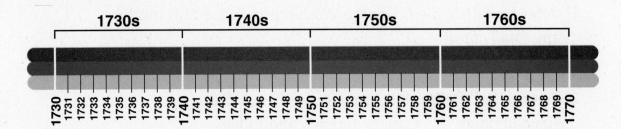

If something happened between 1730 and 1740, you say it happened in the 1730s. If something happened between 1750 and 1760, you say it happened in the _____s. If something happened between 1760 and 1770, you say it happened in the _____s.

Write the decades in the boxes of the time line below. The first one is done for you. Then look at the events on the time line. Write the correct decade on the blank next to each event below. The first one is done for you.

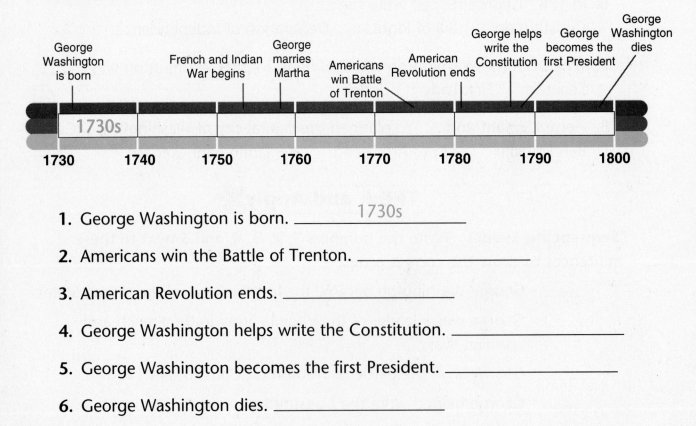

1. George Washington is born. _____1730s_____

2. Americans win the Battle of Trenton. _____

3. American Revolution ends. _____

4. George Washington helps write the Constitution. _____

5. George Washington becomes the first President. _____

6. George Washington dies. _____

The historical map on this page shows the United States when George Washington was President. Study the map. Then use the words in blue print to finish the story.

| Yorktown | Philadelphia | Boston |
| New York City | Washington, D.C. | Trenton |

Americans were angry when the British said they had to pay a tax on tea. So Americans in _____ threw tea into the Atlantic Ocean. In 1776 Americans signed the Declaration of Independence in _____ .

During the American Revolution, George Washington won a Christmas battle at _____ . In 1781 the British army surrendered to Washington at _____ . In 1789 Washington went to _____ to become the first President. As President he planned the country's new capital. The name of the capital is _____ .

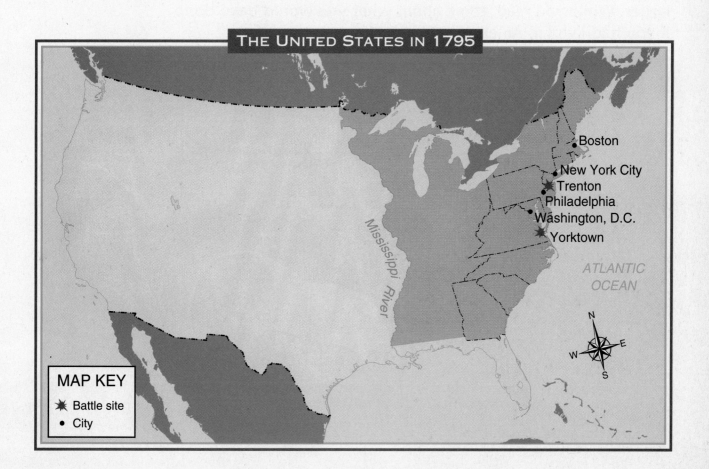

THE UNITED STATES IN 1795

Boston
New York City
Trenton
Philadelphia
Washington, D.C.
Yorktown

Mississippi River

ATLANTIC OCEAN

MAP KEY
✳ Battle site
• City

UNIT 3

THE UNITED STATES GROWS

Imagine you were an explorer in the year 1803. The United States has bought a large piece of a land west of the Mississippi River. Since Americans want to learn about this new land, President Thomas Jefferson wants to send people to explore it. The trip would be long and slow. You would have to cross wide rivers. You would have to climb over very tall mountains.

The United States grew much larger after Thomas Jefferson became President. The United States also became much stronger. From 1812 to 1814, Americans fought and won a second war against Great Britain. After the war more people moved west.

What would you have done if you lived between 1800 and 1840? Would you explore new lands in the West? As you read Unit 3, you will learn how the United States grew stronger and larger. While you read, think about what you would have done if you had lived in America before 1840.

1801
Thomas Jefferson becomes the third President.

1804
Lewis and Clark explore Louisiana.

1812
The War of 1812 begins.

1819
The United States buys Florida from Spain.

1821
Sequoya makes the first Native American alphabet.

1828
Andrew Jackson becomes President.

1837
Mount Holyoke Seminary opens.

1800

1810

1820

1830

1840

1803
The United States buys New Orleans and Louisiana.

1814
Great Britain and the United States sign a peace treaty to end the war.

1835
The Cherokees are forced to move west.

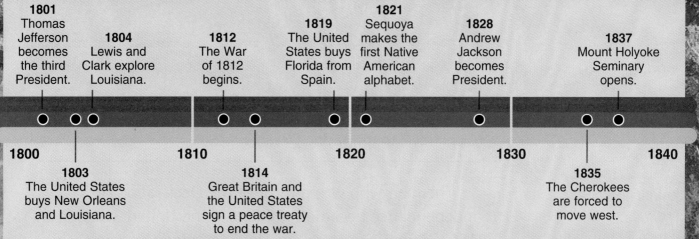

CHAPTER 12 THE UNITED STATES DOUBLES IN SIZE

Think About As You Read

1. Why was New Orleans important to the United States?
2. How did the United States double in size in 1803?
3. How did Lewis and Clark help Thomas Jefferson?

NEW WORDS

crops
Louisiana Purchase
doubled

PEOPLE & PLACES

Napoleon
Meriwether Lewis
William Clark
York
Rocky Mountains
Pacific Ocean
Sacajawea
Oregon

A Native American woman named Sacajawea helped Lewis and Clark travel to the Pacific Ocean.

The man who wrote most of the Declaration of Independence became President of the United States in 1801. Americans voted for Thomas Jefferson to be their third President.

The American Revolution was over. The United States owned all the land east of the Mississippi River except Florida. At first, most Americans lived in the 13 states near the Atlantic Ocean. But every year more Americans moved to the West. By 1800 almost one million Americans lived on the land between the 13 states and the Mississippi River. They built homes and farms. They were starting new states for the United States. In 1803 the United States had 17 states.

Thomas Jefferson

Napoleon

Sometimes Americans moved to land that was being used by Native Americans. Then there were fights between Native Americans and settlers about who would use the land. Many Native Americans were forced to leave their lands.

New Orleans was an important port city near the Gulf of Mexico and the Mississippi River. Many American farmers lived near the Mississippi River. They sent their farm **crops** in boats down the Mississippi River to New Orleans. American farmers sold their farm crops in New Orleans. Ships from New Orleans carried the crops to port cities on the Atlantic Ocean.

Spain owned Louisiana and the city of New Orleans. You read about Louisiana in Chapter 6. Spain allowed American ships to use the port of New Orleans. In 1800 Spain gave New Orleans and Louisiana back to France. New Orleans was a French city again. President Jefferson was worried. Perhaps France would not allow Americans to use the port.

President Jefferson knew that American farmers needed the port of New Orleans. He wanted the United States to own New Orleans. Thomas Jefferson decided to offer to buy the city.

Napoleon was the ruler of France. France was fighting many wars in Europe. Napoleon needed money for the

The United States bought New Orleans from France as part of the Louisiana Purchase in 1803.

UNDER MY WINGS EVERY THING PROSPERS

French wars. Jefferson asked Napoleon to sell New Orleans to the United States. Napoleon said he would sell New Orleans and all of Louisiana to the United States for 15 million dollars. In 1803 the United States paid 15 million dollars for Louisiana. Look at the map of the **Louisiana Purchase** on this page. The United States now owned New Orleans and much land to the west of the Mississippi River. The United States **doubled** in size in 1803.

President Jefferson wanted to learn about the land, plants, and animals of Louisiana. He wanted to know about the Native Americans who lived on this land. Thomas Jefferson asked two men to explore Louisiana. Meriwether Lewis and William Clark became explorers for Thomas Jefferson.

Lewis and Clark started their trip across Louisiana in 1804. About forty men went with them. During the trip Lewis and Clark kept journals. They wrote about the people, plants, animals, and mountains.

An African American traveled with Lewis and Clark. His name was York. York was Clark's slave. He was an excellent

Clark's Journal

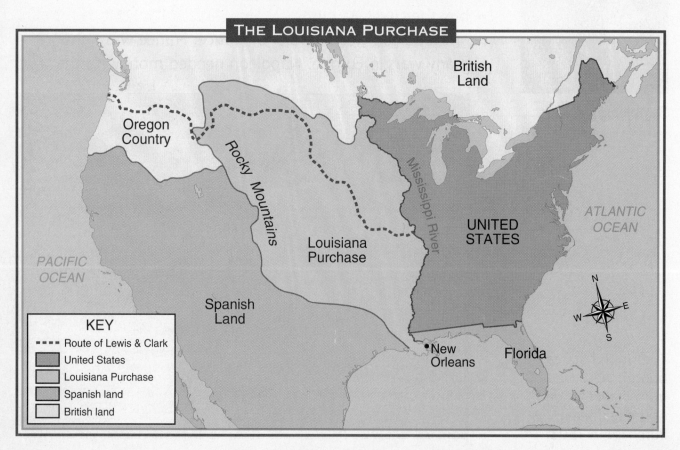

THE LOUISIANA PURCHASE

British Land

Oregon Country

Rocky Mountains

Mississippi River

Louisiana Purchase

UNITED STATES

ATLANTIC OCEAN

PACIFIC OCEAN

Spanish Land

New Orleans

Florida

KEY
- - - - Route of Lewis & Clark
United States
Louisiana Purchase
Spanish land
British land

N E W S

Sacajawea and York helped Lewis and Clark get along with Native Americans.

hunter. York also knew how to get along well with Native Americans. He helped Lewis and Clark become friends with different groups of Native Americans. After the trip ended, Clark gave York his freedom.

During their trip Lewis and Clark reached the Rocky Mountains. Lewis and Clark wanted to cross these mountains and go to the Pacific Ocean. They did not know how to do this. They met a Native American woman who helped them. Her name was Sacajawea. Sacajawea had traveled to the Pacific Ocean before, and she knew the way.

Sacajawea and her husband led Lewis and Clark across the Rocky Mountains. She had a baby boy. She carried the baby on her back. She helped Lewis and Clark find food. Lewis and Clark met Sacajawea's family. Her family gave them horses. After many months, Lewis, Clark, and Sacajawea traveled through Oregon to the Pacific Ocean. The map on page 74 shows the way they traveled to the Pacific Ocean. In 1806 Lewis, Clark, and Sacajawea returned to their homes. They had explored 8,000 miles of land in the West.

Lewis and Clark told Thomas Jefferson about the beautiful land. They made new maps of the West. Thomas Jefferson helped the United States double in size. York, Sacajawea, Lewis, and Clark helped Americans learn about the land in the West.

Read and Remember

True or False   Write **T** next to each sentence that is true. Write **F** next to each sentence that is false.

_____ 1. Thomas Jefferson was the first President of the United States.

_____ 2. New Orleans was an important port for American farmers.

_____ 3. Few Americans moved west to the land between the first 13 states and the Mississippi River.

_____ 4. New Orleans always belonged to France.

_____ 5. Napoleon did not want to sell Louisiana to the United States.

_____ 6. America paid 15 thousand dollars for Louisiana and New Orleans.

_____ 7. The Rocky Mountains are in the West.

_____ 8. York helped Lewis and Clark get along with the Native Americans.

_____ 9. Sacajawea, a Native American woman, led Lewis and Clark across the Rocky Mountains.

Circle the Answer   Draw a circle around the correct answer.

1. Which land east of the Mississippi River was not owned by the United States after the American Revolution?
   Florida   Oregon   Virginia

2. Which country gave Louisiana back to France in 1800?
   Great Britain   Germany   Spain

3. What city did the United States buy in the Louisiana Purchase?
   Boston   New Orleans   Jamestown

4. What did farmers sell in the port city of New Orleans?
   furs   horses   crops

5. Why did Napoleon need money?
   to buy crops   to pay for French wars   to travel west

Think and Apply

Categories   Read the words in each group. Decide how they are alike. Find the best title in blue print for each group. Write the title on the line above each group.

Lewis and Clark   Napoleon   York
Thomas Jefferson   Sacajawea

_____

1. helped write the Declaration of Independence
   third President of the United States
   bought Louisiana from France

_____

2. ruler of France
   wanted to sell Louisiana
   needed money for wars in Europe

_____

3. Native American
   helped Lewis and Clark
   knew how to cross the Rocky Mountains

_____

4. African American slave
   excellent hunter
   friendly with Native Americans

_____

5. explored Louisiana
   kept journals
   made maps of the West

Journal Writing

Look at the list below. If you had gone with Lewis and Clark, which things would you have taken? Choose the five things you think are most important. Then write a paragraph telling why you would have taken each one.

axe   rope   journal   matches   candles
soap   knife   blanket   animal trap   hat

Crossword Puzzle

Each sentence below has a word missing. Choose the missing word for each sentence from the words in blue print. Then write the words in the correct places on the puzzle.

—————— ACROSS ——————

Napoleon   Louisiana   port   Lewis

1. The United States paid 15 million dollars for the _____ Purchase.

2. _____ and Clark explored Louisiana.

3. New Orleans is a _____ on the Gulf of Mexico.

4. _____ was the ruler of France.

—————— DOWN ——————

Jefferson   Oregon   France   Sacajawea

5. Lewis and Clark traveled through _____ to the Pacific Ocean.

6. _____ was fighting many wars in Europe.

7. _____ helped Lewis and Clark cross the Rocky Mountains.

8. _____ wanted to buy New Orleans from France.

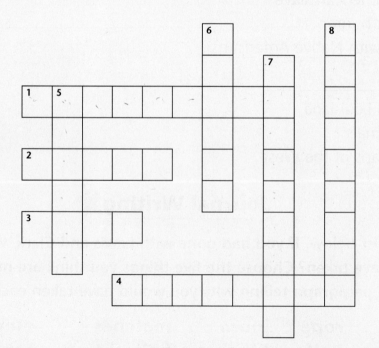

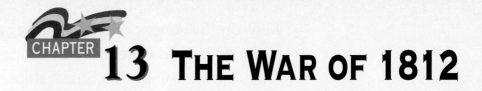

Think About As You Read

1. Why did Americans fight a second war against Great Britain?
2. How did Tecumseh try to help Native Americans?
3. How did the War of 1812 help the United States?

NEW WORDS

captured
freedom of the seas
navy

PEOPLE & PLACES

James Madison
Tecumseh
Dolley Madison
Andrew Jackson

Americans fought the British in the War of 1812 for freedom of the seas.

America and Great Britain were fighting again in the year 1812. Why did Americans fight a second war against the British?

Napoleon, the ruler of France, started a war against Great Britain in 1803. The United States wanted to trade with both Great Britain and France. British ships **captured** many American ships that sailed to France. The French did the same thing to ships that sailed to Great Britain. This made the United States very angry. Americans wanted **freedom of the seas**. "Freedom of the seas" means that ships can sail wherever they want.

The British angered Americans in another way. British ships stopped American ships on the ocean. British captains

79

James Madison

went on the American ships. These captains said that some of the Americans were really British people. They forced these Americans to sail on the British ships. They had to work for the British **navy**. The British forced many Americans to work on British ships. Americans wanted to trade with France. They did not want their ships captured.

The French agreed to freedom of the seas. The British did not. In 1812 the United States began to fight Great Britain for freedom of the seas. This second war against Great Britain was called the War of 1812. James Madison was the President during the War of 1812. He thought the United States would win the war quickly. But the American army and navy were small. The war did not end quickly. Americans fought against the British for more than two years.

During the War of 1812, the United States tried to capture Canada. Canada belonged to Great Britain. American ships captured some of the lakes near Canada. The British army in Canada was strong. The United States could not capture Canada.

Tecumseh was killed in a battle during the War of 1812.

Dolley Madison

A Native American leader named Tecumseh fought for the British during the War of 1812. Tecumseh lived on the land between the eastern states and the Mississippi River. He was angry because each year Americans took more land that belonged to Native Americans. The British promised Tecumseh that they would help the Native Americans get back their land. So Tecumseh and his people fought for Great Britain. He helped them win some battles in Canada. Tecumseh was killed in a battle during the War of 1812.

The American army had burned some buildings in Canada. The British army decided to burn the American capital city, Washington, D.C. President Madison was not in the city when the British army arrived. Dolley Madison, the First Lady, was at home in the White House when Washington, D.C., began to burn.

Dolley Madison stayed in the White House and packed important government papers in a trunk. A beautiful painting of George Washington was in the White House. Dolley asked someone to take it off the wall. The First Lady left Washington, D.C., with the painting and the government papers.

The British marched into Washington, D.C., and burned many government buildings.

Andrew Jackson and his soldiers won the Battle of New Orleans.

Important battles of the War of 1812

Very soon British soldiers came to the White House and burned everything inside. Dolley Madison had saved the painting of George Washington and the important government papers for the United States.

The British wanted to capture the port of New Orleans. Andrew Jackson was a general in the American army. He led 5,000 American soldiers in the Battle of New Orleans. These soldiers included people from Europe, Native Americans, slaves, and free African Americans. General Jackson won the Battle of New Orleans in January 1815. He did not know that two weeks before this battle Great Britain and the United States had signed a peace treaty.

Nothing really changed much because of the War of 1812. Both Great Britain and the United States had won and lost many battles. Neither country won new land in the war. But Great Britain never again fought against the United States. Great Britain and other countries now knew that the United States was strong enough to fight for what it wanted.

Read and Remember ⭐

Circle the Answer   Draw a circle around the correct answer.

1. What country was Great Britain fighting in 1803?
   the United States   France   Spain

2. What did the United States fight Great Britain for in 1812?
   freedom of the seas   freedom of the press   freedom of religion

3. What did the British do to American ships that were sailing to France?
   captured them   burned them   traded with them

4. Who was President during the War of 1812?
   George Washington   Thomas Jefferson   James Madison

5. What did Tecumseh want?
   to be rich   to get back Native American lands   to go to France

6. Who fought for Great Britain during the War of 1812?
   Tecumseh   Andrew Jackson   James Madison

7. What city did the British burn?
   Boston   New Orleans   Washington, D.C.

8. Who saved the painting of George Washington when the British burned Washington, D.C.?
   Dolley Madison   Molly Pitcher   Martha Washington

9. Who won the Battle of New Orleans?
   James Armistead   Ben Franklin   Andrew Jackson

⭐ Journal Writing

It often took months for mail to get anywhere in the United States. Because of the slow mail, Andrew Jackson didn't know that the War of 1812 had ended. He and his soldiers fought the Battle of New Orleans. Imagine how he felt when he learned that the peace treaty had already been signed. Write four or five sentences in your journal that tell how Jackson must have felt.

Think and Apply

Drawing Conclusions Read each pair of sentences. Then look in the box for the conclusion you can make. Write the letter of the conclusion on the blank.

1. British ships captured American ships.
   British captains forced American sailors to work on British ships.

   Conclusion _____

2. Americans wanted Canada to be part of the United States.
   The British army in Canada was strong.

   Conclusion _____

3. African Americans fought in the army.
   People from Europe fought for America.

   Conclusion _____

4. Great Britain and the United States wanted peace.
   Both countries had won and lost many battles.

   Conclusion _____

5. In December 1814 Great Britain and the United States signed a
      peace treaty.
   In January 1815 Jackson won the Battle of New Orleans.

   Conclusion _____

   a. America could not capture Canada.

   b. Great Britain and the United States signed a peace treaty.

   c. Americans fought the British for freedom of the seas.

   d. Andrew Jackson did not know that the war was over.

   e. Many people helped the United States win the war.

14 ANDREW JACKSON

Think About As You Read

1. How did Andrew Jackson become a hero?
2. How did Sequoya help the Cherokees?
3. Why did Osceola fight against the American army?

NEW WORDS

border
Trail of Tears
tariffs

PEOPLE & PLACES

North Carolina
South Carolina
Creeks
Cherokees
Alabama
Sequoya
Oklahoma
Osceola
Seminoles

Andrew Jackson became President in 1828. He was called the "People's President."

Andrew Jackson was the seventh President of our country. He was born near the **border** between North Carolina and South Carolina in 1767. Andrew's father died before Andrew was born. In 1780 Andrew fought for America during the American Revolution. He was 13 years old. Andrew's two brothers died during the American Revolution. His mother also died during the war. Andrew had to live by himself when he was only 14 years old. After the war Andrew studied law and became a lawyer.

Andrew Jackson wanted to help his country during the War of 1812. A large group of Native Americans called the Creeks lived in the South. The Creeks helped the British during the War of 1812. Andrew Jackson led his soldiers against the Creeks. Americans fought the Creeks for many months.

Another group of Native Americans was the Cherokees. They fought with Americans against the Creeks. In March 1814 the Creeks lost an important battle in Alabama. They surrendered to Andrew Jackson and stopped fighting the Americans. The Creeks had to give most of their land in Alabama and Georgia to the Americans. Jackson and his soldiers also fought Native Americans in Florida. Florida belonged to Spain. In 1819 Spain sold Florida to the United States for five million dollars.

Andrew Jackson became a hero. People liked him because he won the battle against the Creeks and the Battle of New Orleans. Andrew Jackson became President of the United States in 1828.

Sequoya was a Cherokee who helped Americans fight the Creeks. The Cherokees spoke their own language. They did not know how to write their language. The Cherokees, like other Native Americans, did not have an alphabet.

The United States fought many battles with Native Americans.

Sequoya decided to help his people learn to read and write. He carefully studied the Cherokee language. By 1821 Sequoya had made an alphabet for the Cherokee language. His alphabet had 86 letters.

Sequoya helped the Cherokees learn to read and write with his alphabet. The Cherokees started the first Native American newspaper. They printed books. The Cherokees started schools. Soon almost every Cherokee could read and write Sequoya's alphabet.

President Jackson believed that Native Americans should move to land west of the Mississippi River. People in the East wanted to have Native American lands. Jackson forced the Native Americans to move across the Mississippi River to Oklahoma in the West. Find Oklahoma on the map on page 132.

Starting in 1835, thousands of Native Americans were forced to move. The Cherokees were forced to move to Oklahoma. Sequoya also moved west. Americans in the East were happy because they had more land. The Native Americans were very unhappy. They did not want to leave their homes, farms,

Sequoya with his Cherokee alphabet

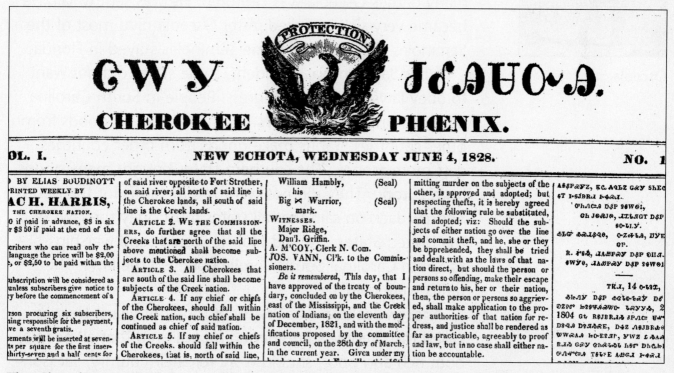

The Cherokees started the first Native American newspaper. It was written in both English and Cherokee.

When Native Americans were forced to move west, their trip was called the Trail of Tears.

Osceola

and villages in the East. Their sad trip to the West was called the **Trail of Tears**. Many Native Americans became sick and died during the long, hard trip.

Osceola was a brave Native American who would not move west. Osceola was the leader of the Seminoles in Florida. He led his people in battles against the American army. After many battles Osceola was captured. He was sent to jail. He became very sick and died. After Osceola died most of the Seminoles moved west. Some Seminoles stayed in Florida.

While Jackson was President, some states did not want to obey laws made by Congress. People in South Carolina did not want to pay **tariffs**. A tariff is a tax on goods from other countries. Tariffs make goods from other countries cost more money. The southern states bought many goods from Europe. They did not want to pay tariffs for the goods. Andrew Jackson said that all states must obey the laws of the United States. He said that he would send warships to South Carolina. South Carolina obeyed the laws. The tariffs were paid.

Andrew Jackson was President for eight years. He was called the "People's President." He believed that all people, both rich and poor, should work for their country. Jackson died in 1845.

★ Read and Remember

Finish the Story   Use the words in the first box to finish the first paragraph. Use the words in the second box to finish the second paragraph. Write the words you choose on the blank lines.

Paragraph 1
British
Spain
five
Florida
Oklahoma
Trail of Tears
tariff

Paragraph 2
newspaper
west
Florida
army
Osceola
alphabet
Mississippi

During the War of 1812, Jackson fought against the _____ .

After the war Jackson fought against Native Americans in _____ .

In 1819 _____ sold Florida to the United States for

_____ million dollars. As President, Jackson said all states must

obey the _____ laws. President Jackson forced Native Americans

to move west to _____ . Their sad trip to the West was called

the _____ .

Two famous Native Americans lived during the time of Andrew Jackson. Sequoya

was a Cherokee. He helped his people by making the first Native American

_____ . The Cherokees used this alphabet to print books and

a _____ . Sequoya was forced to move west across the

_____ River with the other Cherokees. The famous leader of

Native Americans in Florida was _____ . This brave leader would

not move _____ . He fought many battles against the United

States _____ . After Osceola died, most Native Americans in

_____ were forced to move west.

89

Think and Apply

Fact or Opinion   Read each sentence below. Write an **F** next to each sentence that tells a fact. Write an **O** next to each sentence that tells an opinion. You should find six opinions.

_____ 1. Andrew Jackson fought the Creeks.

_____ 2. Andrew Jackson was a kind man.

_____ 3. The United States paid too much money to Spain for Florida.

_____ 4. Sequoya was a Cherokee.

_____ 5. Sequoya spent too much time making the alphabet.

_____ 6. The Cherokees made the first Native American newspaper.

_____ 7. The Cherokee newspaper had many interesting stories.

_____ 8. The United States Congress can write tax laws.

_____ 9. States should not have to pay tariffs.

_____ 10. Andrew Jackson was a better President than Thomas Jefferson.

_____ 11. Jackson believed that Native Americans should move west of the Mississippi River.

_____ 12. The Cherokees moved to Oklahoma.

_____ 13. Osceola wanted to stay in Florida.

_____ 14. Many Native Americans died during the Trail of Tears.

Journal Writing

Imagine that you and your family are Native Americans. You are forced to move west. Think about how you would feel. Write four or five sentences telling about your feelings. Be sure to tell why you feel the way you do.

Skill Builder

Understanding a Picture   Pictures can help you learn about events. The picture below shows Native Americans moving west. Read each pair of sentences. Circle the sentence in each pair that explains the picture. The first one is done for you.

1. Native Americans were happy to move west.

   (Native Americans were sad about moving west.)

2. Few Native Americans were forced to move west.

   Many Native Americans were forced to move west.

3. Native Americans took animals and other things with them.

   Native Americans did not take anything with them.

4. The trip was easy.

   The trip was very hard.

5. Native Americans of all ages moved west.

   Only Native American adults moved west.

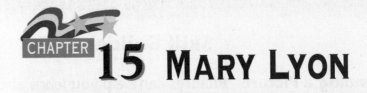
Think About As You Read

1. What were some problems in American education in the 1830s and 1840s?
2. How did Mary Lyon help education for women?
3. How has education for women improved since Mary Lyon lived?

NEW WORDS

public schools
disabilities
education
subjects

PEOPLE & PLACES

Mary Lyon
Emma Willard
Connecticut
Mount Holyoke Seminary
Oberlin College
Ohio

Mary Lyon was an important leader in women's education.

How could the United States become a better country? Many people asked this question during the 1830s and 1840s. Some people believed they could help America by starting more schools for more people. At that time there were not enough **public schools** for the nation's children. There were few schools for children with **disabilities**. It was hard for women to get a good education. In this chapter you will learn how Mary Lyon worked for women's **education**.

Mary Lyon was born in 1797. She lived on a farm in Massachusetts. There were seven children in Mary Lyon's family. All the children in the family had to help with the farm work. Mary Lyon went to school near her house. She was a smart girl and an excellent student. She became a teacher when she was 17 years old.

At that time many people thought that women were not as smart as men. Most men thought women had enough education when they learned to read and write. Women did not study math and science in school. Women were not allowed to go to high school and college. Women could not become doctors or lawyers. Very few women were teachers. Men thought that women should cook, clean, and take care of their families.

One of the first people to work for better education for women was Emma Willard. At that time girls could not go to high school. Emma Willard started the first high school for girls.

Mary Lyon wanted women to have the same chance to learn that men had. She decided to start a college for women. She did not want women to pay a lot of money to be students at her school. She wanted all women to be able to study in her school. Lyon traveled through Massachusetts and Connecticut. Find these states on the

Emma Willard

Both boys and girls were taught to read and write. But girls were not allowed to go to high school or college.

93

map on page 132. She asked people to give her money to build a college for women. Lyon collected thousands of dollars in Massachusetts and Connecticut. In 1836 there was enough money to start building.

The college Mary Lyon built was in Massachusetts. She called it Mount Holyoke Seminary. Mount Holyoke opened in 1837. One hundred women began to study there. Some of the women were rich, but other women were poor. The women learned math, science, languages, and social studies. They studied the same **subjects** that men studied in college.

Mary Lyon was the principal of Mount Holyoke for 12 years. She helped 2,000 women study there. She died in 1849.

Many people learned about Mary Lyon's work. More colleges for women were started. Women were allowed to study in some colleges for men. Oberlin College in Ohio became the first college for men and women.

Today every girl can go to high school. Millions of American women go to college. Mount Holyoke Seminary is now called Mount Holyoke College. Hundreds of women study at Mount Holyoke each year. Mary Lyon was an important leader in women's education.

Mary Lyon opened the first college for women in 1837. It was called Mount Holyoke.

★ Read and Remember

Match Up   Finish each sentence in Group A with words from Group B. Write the letter of the correct answer on the blank line.

Group A

1. In the 1830s there were not enough _____ .

2. There were few schools for children with _____ .

3. Women could not become doctors and _____ .

4. _____ were not allowed to study in colleges.

5. Lyon collected money for her school from people in Massachusetts and _____ .

6. Mary Lyon was _____ at Mount Holyoke Seminary.

Group B

a. Women

b. disabilities

c. the principal

d. lawyers

e. public schools

f. Connecticut

Think and Apply ★

Sequencing Events   Write the numbers **1**, **2**, **3**, and **4** next to these sentences to show the correct order.

_____ Mary Lyon collected money to start a college for women.

_____ More colleges for women were started.

_____ Mount Holyoke opened in 1837.

_____ In 1836 there was enough money to build Mount Holyoke.

★ Journal Writing

What can women do today that they were not allowed to do in 1837? Write a paragraph in your journal that tells how women's lives have changed. Use at least three ideas from the chapter.

Crossword Puzzle

Each sentence below has a word missing. Choose the missing word for each sentence from the words in blue print. Then write the words in the correct places on the puzzle.

——————————————— ACROSS ———————————————

Oberlin   teachers   colleges   collected

1. Mary Lyon _____ money to build a college.

2. _____ was the first college for men and women.

3. Today millions of women study in _____ .

4. When Mary Lyon was young, few women were _____ .

——————————————— DOWN ———————————————

subjects   high   Holyoke   student

5. The first college for women was Mount _____ Seminary.

6. Mary Lyon was an excellent _____ in school.

7. Emma Willard started the first _____ school for girls.

8. Math, science, and social studies are school _____ .

The historical map on this page shows how the United States had grown larger by 1819. Study the map. Then use the words in blue print to finish the story.

Canada   New Orleans   Oregon
Florida   Washington, D.C.   Louisiana

   The United States bought _____ and New Orleans

from France in 1803. Lewis and Clark explored the area. They traveled

through _____ Country to the Pacific Ocean.

   During the War of 1812, the United States tried to capture

_____ . The British burned the White House and other

buildings in _____ . Andrew Jackson won the Battle of

_____ at the end of the war. In 1819 the United States

paid Spain five million dollars for _____ .

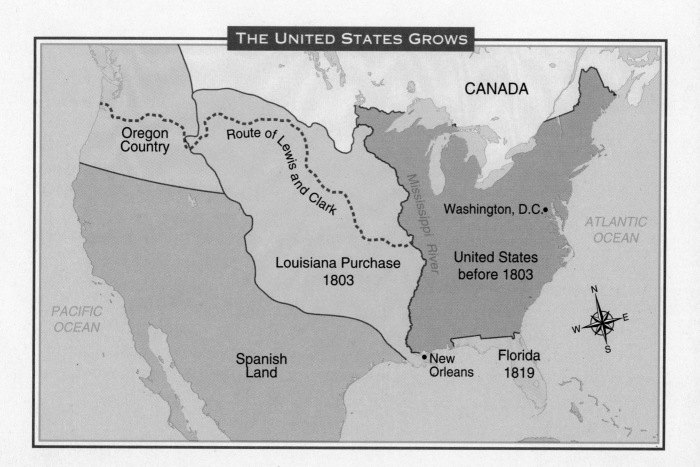

THE UNITED STATES GROWS

UNIT 4 · THE NATION GROWS AND DIVIDES

Imagine living in the United States in 1860. Everyone believes there will be a war between the northern states and the southern states. You must choose a side to fight for in this war. You may have to fight against your own brothers during the war. You might fight against your best friend. Thousands will die during the Civil War.

The years between 1821 and 1865 were years of great change. The nation grew much larger. Many Americans moved west. The problem of slavery also grew. The northern states did not want slaves. The southern states said they needed slaves. In 1861 the terrible Civil War began.

What would you do if you lived between 1821 and 1865? Would you move west? Would you fight for the northern states or for the southern states? As you read Unit 4, think about what choices you would make.

1821
Stephen Austin starts an American colony in Texas.

1836
Texas wins independence from Mexico.

1845
Texas becomes a state.

1848
The United States wins the Mexican War.

1850
California becomes a state.

1861
Abe Lincoln becomes President.

1865
The Civil War ends.

1820

1830

1840

1850

1860

1870

1843
People go to Oregon on the Oregon Trail.

1846
A peace treaty is signed about Oregon.

1859
Oregon becomes a state.

1861
The Civil War begins.

Think About As You Read

1. Why did Americans want to settle in Texas?
2. What problems did Americans and Mexicans have in Texas?
3. How did Texas become free from Mexico?

NEW WORDS

fort
Texas Revolution
republic

PEOPLE & PLACES

Moses Austin
Stephen Austin
Mexicans
Texans
José Antonio Navarro
Lorenzo de Zavala
Santa Anna
Alamo
Suzanna Dickenson
Sam Houston
San Jacinto River
Republic of Texas

Many Americans and Mexicans moved to Texas in the 1800s.

Mexico belonged to Spain for 300 years. In 1821 Mexico became an independent country. At that time, Texas was part of Mexico.

Moses Austin wanted to start a colony for Americans in Texas. He died before he could start the colony. His son, Stephen Austin, decided to continue his father's plan to settle Texas. Few Mexicans lived in Texas. So the leaders of Mexico wanted Americans to move to Texas.

Stephen Austin started an American colony in Texas in 1821. The settlers liked Texas. Land was cheaper there. African Americans, German Americans, and Asian Americans moved to Texas. Jewish Americans and new Americans

Stephen Austin

from Europe also settled in Texas. More people from Mexico went to live in Texas. By 1830 there were many more Americans than Mexicans in Texas. People who live in Texas are called Texans.

Mexico's leaders were worried about Texas. They were afraid Americans might want Texas to become part of the United States. So in 1830 Mexico made a new law. The law said that Americans could no longer come to live in Texas. Americans in Texas did not like this law.

Texans did not like other Mexican laws. They did not like the tax laws. They did not like the law that said they could not bring slaves into Texas. Texans did not like the law that said they must speak Spanish. Another Mexican law said settlers must be Catholics. The Texans wanted to help write laws for Texas. Mexico would not let the settlers make laws for Texas.

Mexico was also angry with the new settlers. Mexico was angry because very few settlers had become Mexicans. The settlers brought slaves to Texas. Few Texans spoke Spanish. Many Texans were not Catholic. Mexican soldiers went to Texas to force the Texans to obey Mexican laws. This made

Austin sold land to many families who wanted to move to Texas.

José Antonio Navarro

Lorenzo de Zavala

Texas flag

Santa Anna and his soldiers attacked the Texans at the Alamo.

the Texans angry and unhappy. They did not want Mexican soldiers in Texas.

The Texans decided that Texas should be independent from Mexico. In March 1836 the leaders of Texas wrote a declaration of independence. This declaration said that Texas was no longer part of Mexico.

American Texans were not the only people who wanted Texas to be independent. Some Mexican Texans also wanted an independent Texas. José Antonio Navarro was a Mexican who was born in Texas. He was a friend of Stephen Austin. He signed the Texas Declaration of Independence. He later helped write a new constitution for Texas. Lorenzo de Zavala was born in Mexico. He came to live in Texas with his family. De Zavala also signed the Texas Declaration of Independence. He told all Texans to fight for freedom.

Santa Anna, the Mexican president, did not want the Texans to be independent. He led his army against the Texans. There were about 180 Texan soldiers in a mission called the Alamo. The Texans used the Alamo as a **fort**. Santa Anna and 3,000 Mexican soldiers attacked the Alamo.

Santa Anna surrendered to Sam Houston after the battle at the San Jacinto River.

Santa Anna

Suzanna Dickenson

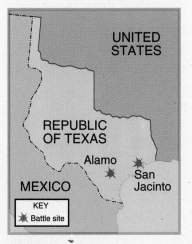

Republic of Texas

The Texans were brave and would not surrender. They fought for many days. Santa Anna won the Battle of the Alamo. Every Texan soldier was killed.

Some of the Texan soldiers had brought their wives and children to the Alamo. One of these wives was Suzanna Dickenson. After the battle, Santa Anna sent her to tell other Texans not to fight against Mexico.

Sam Houston became the commander in chief of the Texas army. He learned about the Battle of the Alamo from Dickenson. Sam told his soldiers to remember the brave people who died at the Alamo.

On April 21, 1836, the Texans fought Santa Anna again. They fought at the San Jacinto River. "Remember the Alamo!" Sam Houston's soldiers shouted as they fought the Mexicans. The battle lasted only 18 minutes. The Texans won. Santa Anna surrendered to Sam Houston. Texas was now free. The Texans called their war against Mexico the **Texas Revolution**.

Texas was no longer part of Mexico, and Texas was not part of the United States. Texas became a **republic**. A republic is an independent country. Sam Houston became the first president of the Republic of Texas.

Texans wanted Texas to become part of the United States. But they would have to wait almost ten more years before Texas would become a state.

⭐ Read and Remember

Finish Up Choose a word in blue print to finish each sentence. Write the word or words you choose on the correct blank.

republic   Sam Houston   Santa Anna   Texas Revolution
Alamo   San Jacinto   de Zavala   Stephen Austin

1. _____ started an American colony in Texas.

2. José Antonio Navarro and Lorenzo _____ were Mexican Texans who signed the Texas Declaration of Independence.

3. The commander in chief of the army and the first president of Texas was _____ .

4. The leader of the Mexican army was President _____ .

5. The war for Texan independence was called the _____ .

6. About 180 Texan soldiers died at the _____ .

7. Santa Anna surrendered at the _____ River.

8. After the war, Texas was an independent _____ .

True or False Write **T** next to each sentence that is true. Write **F** next to each sentence that is false.

_____ 1. In 1821 Mexico became an independent country.

_____ 2. José Antonio Navarro started an American colony in Texas.

_____ 3. By 1830 there were more Mexicans than Americans in Texas.

_____ 4. Mexico would not let the Texan settlers write laws.

_____ 5. Texans wrote a declaration of independence to say that Texas was no longer a part of Mexico.

_____ **6.** Texans won the Battle of the Alamo.

_____ **7.** Suzanna Dickenson told people about the Battle of the Alamo.

_____ **8.** Texas became a republic after the Texas Revolution.

Think and Apply

Understanding Different Points of View   The Mexicans and the Americans had different points of view about Texas. Read each pair of sentences below. Write **Texan** next to the sentences that show the Texan point of view. Write **Mexican** next to the sentences that show the Mexican point of view.

_____ **1.** People in Texas should obey Mexican laws.

_____ People in Texas should write their own laws.

_____ **2.** Everyone in Texas must be Catholic.

_____ Americans in Texas do not have to be Catholic.

_____ **3.** Americans can bring slaves to Texas.

_____ Americans cannot have slaves in Texas.

_____ **4.** Americans should speak Spanish in Texas.

_____ Americans can speak English in Texas.

_____ **5.** Texas should be independent.

_____ Texas must belong to Mexico.

Journal Writing

Read about the Texas Revolution again. Why was "Remember the Alamo!" a good thing to shout at the battle near the San Jacinto River? Write a paragraph that tells why. Include at least two reasons.

CHAPTER 17

THE UNITED STATES GROWS LARGER

Think About As You Read

1. What was Manifest Destiny?
2. How did the Mexican War help the United States grow larger?
3. How did Mexican Americans help the United States?

NEW WORDS

Manifest Destiny
citizens
Mexican Cession
Gadsden Purchase
property

PEOPLE & PLACES

James Polk
Rio Grande
Mexico City
Nevada
Utah
Arizona
Mexican Americans

When the flag of the Republic of Texas was lowered, Texas became the twenty-eighth state in the United States.

In Chapter 16 you read that Texans won their war against Mexico and started a republic. Santa Anna had surrendered to the Texans. But Mexican leaders did not accept his surrender. The Mexicans said that Texas was still part of Mexico. Texans wanted to become part of the United States. The Mexicans said there would be a war if Texas became part of the United States.

Many Americans wanted Texas to become a state. They believed in an idea called **Manifest Destiny**. Manifest Destiny meant the United States should rule all the land between the Atlantic Ocean and the Pacific Ocean. This idea also meant that the United States should become a larger and stronger country.

James Polk

Texas land claimed by Mexico

In 1845 the United States Congress voted for Texas to become the twenty-eighth state. During that same year, James Polk became President. The new President believed in Manifest Destiny. He wanted the United States to own all the land to the Pacific Ocean.

In 1846 a war started between the United States and Mexico. The two countries did not agree on the border for Texas. The United States said a river called the Rio Grande was the southern border for Texas. Mexico said Texas should be smaller. The Mexicans said that much of the land northeast of the Rio Grande belonged to Mexico. Find the Rio Grande on the map on this page.

The United States and Mexico sent soldiers to the Rio Grande. The soldiers began to fight. This war was called the Mexican War. During the war American soldiers captured California and New Mexico. The Mexican soldiers were brave. They did not stop fighting. Americans and Mexicans continued to fight. American soldiers went into Mexico. They captured Mexico City, the capital of Mexico. In 1848 the Mexicans surrendered. The war was over.

American soldiers stand in the center of Mexico City after capturing this capital city of Mexico.

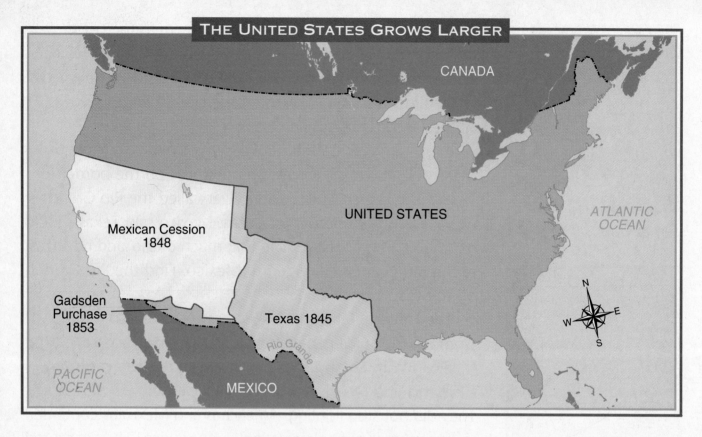

The leaders of the United States and Mexico signed a peace treaty in 1848. The peace treaty said there was peace between the United States and Mexico. The treaty said that Texas belonged to the United States. Both countries agreed that the Rio Grande was the border between Texas and Mexico. The treaty also said that Mexicans in the Southwest could become American **citizens**. The United States gave Mexico 15 million dollars for land taken during the war.

The land that the United States got in 1848 was called the **Mexican Cession**. Find the Mexican Cession on the map above. California, Nevada, Utah, Arizona, and New Mexico were five new states made from the Mexican Cession. The United States now owned land from the Atlantic Ocean to the Pacific Ocean.

Americans wanted a railroad across the southern part of the United States. The land south of the Mexican Cession was a good place for a railroad. In 1853 the United States gave Mexico 10 million dollars for the land in the **Gadsden Purchase**. Find the Gadsden Purchase on the map above. Years later, Americans built a railroad across the Gadsden Purchase.

The Mexicans in the Southwest became American citizens after the Mexican War. They were called Mexican Americans.

Mexican Americans helped their new country. They taught Americans how to grow food on land where there was little rain. Mexican Americans helped build railroads for the United States. They helped other Americans look for gold and silver in the Southwest.

Mexican Americans helped the United States change a law that was unfair to women. Before the Mexican War, a married American woman could not own **property**. Her husband owned everything. Mexican law was fairer to women. Mexican women owned property together with their husbands. After the Mexican War, Americans changed their law so that women could own property with their husbands.

The land between the Atlantic Ocean and the Pacific Ocean belonged to the United States. The United States had become a strong country with a lot of new land and many new people.

Mexican Americans in the Southwest taught Americans many things, including how to be cowboys.

⭐ Read and Remember

Circle the Answer   Draw a circle around the correct answer.

1. Which President believed in Manifest Destiny?
   James Madison   Andrew Jackson   James Polk

2. When did Texas become a state?
   1776   1845   1900

3. What city did the American soldiers capture?
   Rio Grande   Alamo   Mexico City

4. How much did the United States pay for the Mexican Cession?
   5 million dollars   15 million dollars   30 million dollars

5. Which three states were among the five made from the Mexican Cession?
   California, New Mexico, Arizona   New York, New Jersey, Florida
   Texas, Oregon, Oklahoma

6. Which river became the border for Texas?
   Mississippi River   St. Lawrence River   Rio Grande

7. What land did the United States buy in 1853?
   Louisiana Purchase   Gadsden Purchase   Florida

8. Why did the United States want the Gadsden Purchase?
   for oil   for a railroad   for a park

Skill Builder ⭐

Reviewing Map Directions   Look back at the map on page 108. Draw a circle around the word that finishes the sentence.

1. The Gadsden Purchase is _____ of Mexico.
   east   south   north

2. The Pacific Ocean is _____ of the Mexican Cession.
   southeast   east   west

3. The Rio Grande is _____ of the Gadsden Purchase.
   south   southwest   east

4. The Mexican Cession is _____ of the Gadsden Purchase.

    south   southeast   north

5. Mexico is _____ of the United States.

    south   north   west

6. Texas is _____ of the Gadsden Purchase.

    east   southwest   west

7. Canada is _____ of Mexico.

    west   north   east

 # Think and Apply

Cause and Effect Match each cause on the left with an effect on the right. Write the letter of the effect on the correct blank.

Cause

1. In 1845 many Americans believed their country should be larger, so _____

2. Texas became a state, so _____

3. The United States captured Mexico City, so _____

4. In 1848 the United States got land in the Mexican Cession, so _____

5. Americans wanted to build a railroad across the southern part of the United States, so _____

Effect

a. they paid Mexico 10 million dollars for land in the Gadsden Purchase.

b. Mexico said there would be a war with the United States.

c. the country's borders went from the Atlantic Ocean to the Pacific Ocean.

d. the United States Congress voted for Texas to become the twenty-eighth state.

e. Mexico surrendered.

Journal Writing

Mexican Americans became citizens of the United States after the Mexican War. Write a paragraph in your journal that tells how Mexican Americans have helped the United States.

Crossword Puzzle

Each sentence below has a word missing. Choose the missing word for each sentence from the words in blue print. Then write the words in the correct places on the puzzle.

─────── ACROSS ───────

treaty   California   Manifest   railroad   Gadsden

1. _____ was part of the Mexican Cession.

2. In 1848 the United States and Mexico signed a peace _____ .

3. In 1853 the United States bought land in the _____ Purchase.

4. _____ Destiny meant the United States should own all land between the Atlantic Ocean and the Pacific Ocean.

5. Americans built a _____ across the land bought in the Gadsden Purchase.

─────── DOWN ───────

Nevada   War   law   Mexican   citizens

6. Mexican _____ allowed married women to own property.

7. The Mexican _____ started after Texas became a state.

8. Mexicans of the Southwest could become American _____ .

9. _____ was part of the Mexican Cession.

10. The land that the United States got from Mexico in 1848 was the _____ Cession.

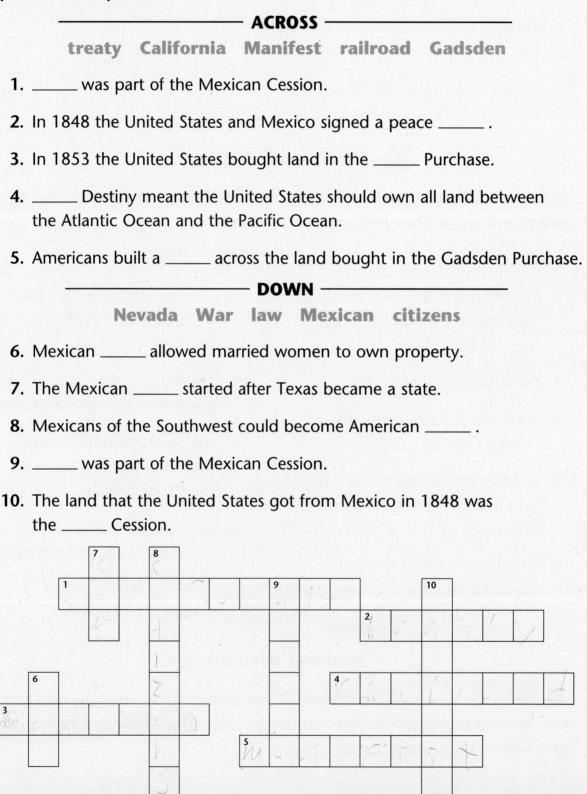

CHAPTER 18

ON TO OREGON AND CALIFORNIA

Think About As You Read

1. Why did people want to go to Oregon?
2. How did people travel to Oregon in the 1840s?
3. What happened after gold was found in California?

NEW WORDS

covered wagons
oxen
wagon train
Oregon Trail
coast
gold rush
pass

PEOPLE & PLACES

Independence, Missouri
Washington
Idaho
James Marshall
China
James Beckwourth
Beckwourth Pass

Families that traveled to Oregon had to cross the Rocky Mountains.

"On to Oregon! Let's move to Oregon!" said thousands of Americans in the 1840s. Oregon had lots of trees for building new houses. Oregon had good land for farming. Soon thousands of Americans moved west to build new homes and farms in the Oregon country.

The trip to Oregon was long and slow. There were no roads across the United States to Oregon. Families traveled to Oregon in **covered wagons**. Horses and **oxen** pulled the covered wagons. In 1843 many families in 120 covered wagons met in Independence, Missouri. These 120 covered wagons made a **wagon train**. The covered wagons traveled together across the Great Plains and the Rocky Mountains to Oregon.

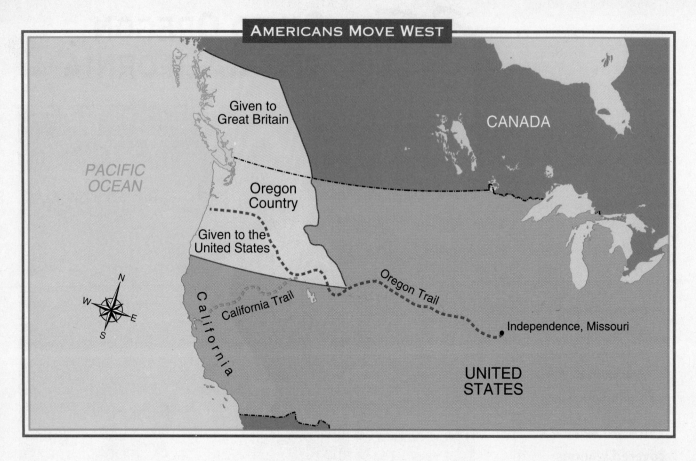

What was it like to travel on the wagon train? All families woke up very early every day. Then people traveled as many hours as they could. At night they slept on the floors of their covered wagons. When it rained, wagon wheels got stuck in mud. Sometimes wagons turned over. Then people inside the wagons were hurt or killed. It was hard to find food on the way to Oregon. Many families were hungry. The long trip to Oregon took about six months.

At last the families reached the Oregon country. They had traveled 2,000 miles. The families had followed a trail to Oregon. It became known as the **Oregon Trail**. Find the Oregon Trail on the map above. Thousands of people came to Oregon on the Oregon Trail. These people were some of the first Americans to settle along the Pacific **coast**.

The Oregon country was much bigger than our state of Oregon today. The Oregon country included part of Canada. Great Britain and the United States had shared the Oregon country for many years. The two nations could not decide on a way to divide Oregon. President Polk wanted

Oregon to be part of the United States. Many people thought Great Britain and the United States would fight for Oregon. This time the two nations did not fight. President Polk signed a peace treaty with Great Britain about Oregon in 1846.

The treaty said that northern Oregon was part of Canada. Canada and northern Oregon belonged to Great Britain. Southern Oregon became part of the United States. Later the states of Oregon, Washington, and Idaho were made from the southern part of the Oregon country.

The United States government gave free farm land to families that moved to the state of Oregon. Many Americans came to Oregon on the Oregon Trail for free land. In 1859 the United States Congress voted for Oregon to become a state.

While thousands of Americans were moving to the state of Oregon, other Americans were rushing to California. One day in 1848, a man named James Marshall found pieces of gold in a river in California. Soon everyone knew that James Marshall had found gold.

People from all over the United States began moving to California. "Gold! Gold! Gold! There's gold in California," said Americans as they traveled to California. They wanted

Many people moved to California to look for gold.

James Beckwourth found a mountain pass that made it easier for Americans to travel west.

to find gold and become rich. We say that California had a **gold rush** in 1848 and 1849 because thousands of people went to find gold.

The gold rush brought many kinds of people to California. Many people came from Europe to look for gold in California. People came from China to find gold. Free African Americans also moved to California.

James Beckwourth made it easier for many people to travel west to California. Beckwourth was an African American. He moved west and lived with Native Americans. Tall mountains in the West made it hard to go to California. Beckwourth looked and looked for an easier way to go across the mountains. At last Beckwourth found a **pass** through the mountains. Many people used this pass to reach California. Today that pass through the mountains is called the Beckwourth Pass.

Some people were lucky in California. They found gold and became rich. Most people did not find gold. Many people stayed in California. They built farms and factories. They started new cities. They built stores and houses. By 1850, 90,000 people were living in California. The United States Congress voted for California to become a state in 1850.

The California gold rush brought thousands of settlers to California. The Oregon Trail brought thousands of Americans to the Northwest. Every year more Americans moved west to California and Oregon.

Read and Remember

Finish the Sentence   Draw a circle around the date, word, or words that finish each sentence.

1. Thousands of Americans went to the Oregon country in the _____ .
   1820s   1830s   1840s

2. In 1846 the northern part of the Oregon country became part of _____ .
   the United States   Canada   Washington

3. Families that moved to Oregon were given free _____ .
   wagons   houses   farm land

4. In 1848 and 1849, Americans rushed to California to find _____ .
   silver   gold   trees

5. California became a state in _____ .
   1850   1859   1860

Think and Apply

Categories   Read the words in each group. Decide how they are alike. Find the best title in blue print for each group. Write the title on the line above each group.

James Beckwourth   California   Oregon Trail   Gold Rush

1. _____
   1848 and 1849
   people searched for gold
   thousands came to California

2. _____
   African American
   lived in the West
   found a pass

3. _____
   horses and oxen
   covered wagons
   went to Oregon

4. _____
   gold rush
   built farms
   started cities

Skill Builder

Reading a Historical Map The map below shows how the United States became a large country. Study each area and when it became part of the United States.

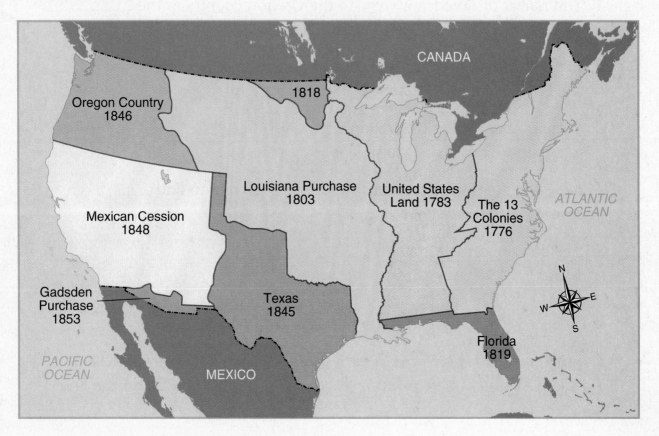

Use the map to answer each question.

1. What land made up the United States in 1776?
   Texas   The 13 Colonies   Louisiana

2. What southeast land belonged to Spain until 1819?
   Oregon Country   Texas   Florida

3. What land did the United States buy in 1803?
   Mexican Cession   Louisiana Purchase   Texas

4. Which northwest land became part of the United States in 1846?
   Oregon Country   Florida   Louisiana Purchase

5. Which land did the United States buy in 1853?
   Gadsden Purchase   Oregon Country   Texas

On plantations in the South, slaves did most of the farm work.

Think About As You Read

1. Why were there more slaves in the South than in the North?
2. What were two reasons why the South became angry with the North?
3. What did the South do after Abraham Lincoln became President?

NEW WORDS

quarreling
plantations
sugar cane
escape
products
Confederate States of America

PEOPLE & PLACES

North
South
Harriet Tubman
Abraham Lincoln
Confederate States

The United States had become a large country after the Mexican War. But things were not going well in the United States. The northern states were **quarreling** with the southern states. The northern states were called the North, and the southern states were called the South. Why did the North and South quarrel?

In Chapter 5 you learned how the English started colonies in America. Do you remember that in 1619 the English brought African slaves to America? A slave is a person who belongs to another person. A slave is not free.

At first, there were slaves both in the North and in the South. But farms were small in the North. The North had many factories. Most people there did not need slaves to work on their farms and in factories. There were fewer slaves in the North.

119

In the South some people owned very large farms called **plantations**. The owners grew cotton, **sugar cane**, and tobacco on their plantations. Plantation owners needed many workers. They bought slaves to do the work. The plantation owners in the South thought they could not grow crops without slaves.

After the Mexican War, more Americans moved to the West. People from the South started new plantations in the West. They wanted to bring their slaves. The northern states did not want slavery in the West.

The North and South began to quarrel. In the North many people said that all people should be free. They said that it was not right for one person to own another person. In the South people said that the Constitution allowed slavery. People in the South said that people in the North should not tell them what to do. The people in the North wanted to make new laws against slavery in the West. This made the South very angry.

Plantation owners in the South bought and sold slaves.

Many slaves escaped to freedom in the North.

Harriet Tubman

The South was worried because many Americans were trying to end slavery. Some people wrote books and newspapers that told why slavery was wrong. Some people gave speeches against slavery. Other people helped slaves run away from their owners. Harriet Tubman was one of the people who helped slaves become free. Harriet Tubman had been a slave herself. She had run away to the North. In the North she became a free woman. She went back to the South and helped slaves **escape** to Canada. In Canada the slaves were free. Harriet Tubman helped hundreds of slaves get their freedom.

Southerners were also angry about a tariff law. You read about tariffs in Chapter 14. There were many factories in the North. People made shoes, clothes, and other things in factories. There were very few factories in the South. People in the South had to buy many things from the North and from Europe. Northerners wanted Southerners to pay extra money, or a tariff, for everything they bought from Europe. The tariff made things from Europe more expensive. Factories in the North also made their **products** more expensive. The South did not like paying more for things made in both Europe and the North.

Abraham Lincoln came from a poor family.

Abraham Lincoln

In 1861 a man named Abraham Lincoln became the President of the United States. What kind of man was Abe Lincoln? He came from a poor family. Abe lived very far from school when he was young. So he only went to school for about one year. He learned as much as he could by reading books. Abe grew up to be very tall, thin, and strong. He became a lawyer. Many people liked him because he was honest and smart.

Abe Lincoln believed that slavery was wrong. He said that slavery should not be allowed in the West. The North liked what Abe said, but the South did not. The South was afraid that Abe would work to end slavery everywhere.

Eleven southern states decided that they no longer wanted to be part of the United States. In 1861 they started a new country. They called their country the **Confederate States of America**.

Abe Lincoln was very unhappy. He said that the United States must be one country, not two. Would the United States and the Confederate States become one country again? Would it take a war to get them together? Chapter 20 will give you the answers.

★ Read and Remember

True or False   Write **T** next to each sentence that is true. Write **F** next to each sentence that is false.

_____ 1. The North had more factories than the South.

_____ 2. People grew cotton, sugar cane, and tobacco in the South.

_____ 3. Slaves worked on large plantations in the North.

_____ 4. Harriet Tubman only helped three slaves escape.

_____ 5. The North said that slavery should be allowed in the West.

_____ 6. Abe Lincoln became President in 1861.

_____ 7. Thirteen northern states left the United States and became the Confederate States of America.

Think and Apply ★

Fact or Opinion   Read each sentence below. Write an **F** next to each sentence that tells a fact. Write an **O** next to each sentence that tells an opinion. You should find three opinions.

_____ 1. The Constitution allowed slavery.

_____ 2. The North had more factories than the South.

_____ 3. It is wrong to own slaves.

_____ 4. The South had to pay a tariff on products from Europe.

_____ 5. The tariff laws were not fair.

_____ 6. Abe Lincoln did not want slavery in the West.

_____ 7. People in the South were the best farmers.

★ Journal Writing

Harriet Tubman helped slaves escape. Why do you think she helped them? Write a paragraph in your journal.

Skill Builder

Reading a Bar Graph Graphs are drawings that help you compare facts. The graph on this page is a **bar graph**. It shows facts using bars of different lengths. The bar graph below shows the number of people who lived in the United States in 1860.

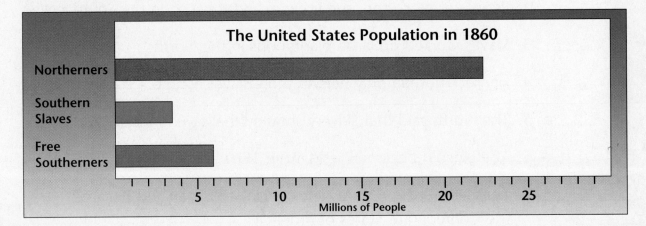

The United States Population in 1860

Northerners

Southern Slaves

Free Southerners

5   10   15   20   25

Millions of People

Use the bar graph to answer each question.

1. How many people lived in the North?
   $3\frac{1}{2}$ million   6 million   22 million

2. How many slaves lived in the South?
   $3\frac{1}{2}$ million   6 million   22 million

3. Which group had the largest population?
   Northerners   Free Southerners   Southern Slaves

Make a Graph In 1863 there were 11 Confederate states. There were 24 northern states. Draw a bar for each group of states on the graph below.

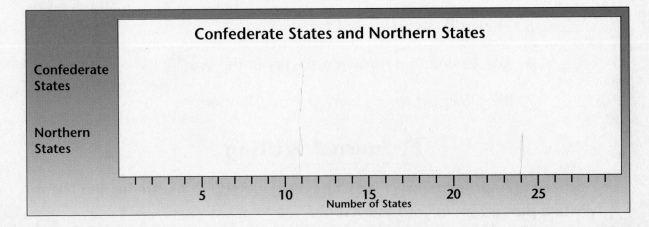

Confederate States and Northern States

Confederate States

Northern States

5   10   15   20   25

Number of States

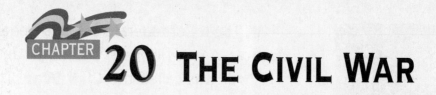
20 THE CIVIL WAR

Think About As You Read

1. What did the South fight for during the Civil War?
2. What did the North fight for during the Civil War?
3. Why did Robert E. Lee surrender?

NEW WORDS

Union
Confederates
Civil War
goal
destroyed
rebuild

PEOPLE & PLACES

Fort Sumter
Robert E. Lee
Clara Barton
Ulysses S. Grant
Richmond

Many soldiers from both the North and the South were killed in the Civil War.

The South had started a new country called the Confederate States of America. President Lincoln did not want the North to fight against the South. He wanted the South to become part of the United States again. The **Union** is another name for the United States. The South did not want a war. But the South did not want to be part of the Union.

The United States Army owned a fort called Fort Sumter in South Carolina. South Carolina was one of the Confederate States. People who lived in the Confederate States were called **Confederates**. They said that the United States must give Fort Sumter to the Confederate States of America. But Union soldiers would not surrender Fort Sumter.

125

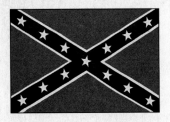

Confederate battle flag

Robert E. Lee

In 1861 Confederate soldiers began to shoot at Fort Sumter. A war between the North and South had begun. This war was called the **Civil War**. The Civil War lasted four years. People in the South fought to have their own country, the Confederate States of America. The North fought so that all states would remain in the Union.

The Confederates thought they would win. They had many good army generals and brave soldiers. But the North was stronger than the South. The North had more people and more soldiers. The North had more money to pay for a war. The North had more railroads. Union soldiers traveled on these railroads to many places. The North had more factories, too. Northern factories made guns for the war.

Robert E. Lee was the leader of the Confederate army. Robert E. Lee loved the United States. He did not like slavery. He also loved his own state of Virginia. President Lincoln wanted Robert E. Lee to lead the Union army. But Robert E. Lee would not fight against his family and friends in Virginia. Instead, he became the leader of the Confederate army. Lee was

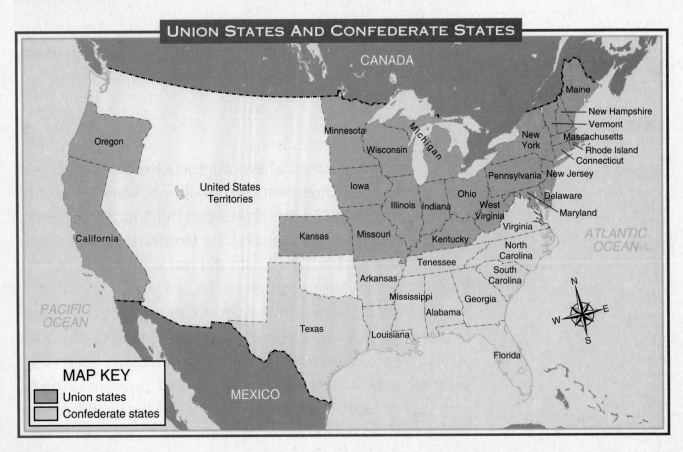

UNION STATES AND CONFEDERATE STATES

CANADA

Maine
New Hampshire
Vermont
Minnesota
Massachusetts
Wisconsin
New York
Rhode Island
Connecticut
Pennsylvania
New Jersey
Oregon
Iowa
Ohio
Delaware
Illinois
Indiana
West Virginia
Maryland
United States Territories
Virginia
ATLANTIC OCEAN
California
Kansas
Missouri
Kentucky
North Carolina
Tenessee
South Carolina
Arkansas
Georgia
Mississippi
Alabama
PACIFIC OCEAN
Texas
Louisiana
Florida

MEXICO

MAP KEY
Union states
Confederate states

Many African Americans joined the Union army and fought in the Civil War.

Clara Barton

Major Civil War battles

an excellent leader. He led the Confederate army for four long years.

President Lincoln had a **goal**. His goal was for the North and South to be one nation. He decided to help the Union win by working to end slavery. In 1863 he gave orders that said all slaves in the Confederate States were free. Many African American slaves left the South. Thousands of African Americans joined the Union army. They fought in many important battles of the Civil War.

Women in the North and South helped during the war. They took care of the farms and factories. Some women became spies. Many women became nurses. Clara Barton became one of the most famous Union nurses. She traveled to places where there were terrible battles. Clara Barton cared for soldiers who were hurt.

At the start of the Civil War, the South won many battles. After two years the South lost more and more battles. Most of the Civil War battles were fought in the South. The fighting **destroyed** houses, cities, and plantations in the South.

Ulysses S. Grant was the leader of the Union army. He won many battles. In 1865 the Union soldiers captured

President Abraham Lincoln was shot soon after the end of the Civil War.

Ulysses S. Grant

Richmond, Virginia. Richmond was the capital of the Confederate States. Then Robert E. Lee knew that the Confederates could not win the war. There was very little food to eat in the South. Lee's army was hungry and weak. He did not want more people to die in the war. Lee surrendered to Grant in April 1865. The war was over. Plans were made to return the Confederate States to the Union. Robert E. Lee returned to Virginia. He told the South to help the United States become a strong country.

President Lincoln was glad that the United States was one nation again. He was also sad. Almost 600,000 soldiers in the North and South had been killed. Thousands of other soldiers were badly hurt.

President Lincoln had new goals when the war ended. He wanted Americans to work together to **rebuild** the South. He wanted Americans in the North and South to like each other again.

President Lincoln never reached these goals. He was shot in the head five days after the Civil War ended. Abraham Lincoln died the next day. Americans in the North and South were sad because a great leader was dead.

People in the North and the South were united once again. It would take many more years to end the anger between the North and the South. But together they would continue to make the United States a great nation.

Read and Remember

Write the Answer   Write a sentence to answer each question.

1. What did the North fight for in the Civil War? _____

_____

2. What did the South fight for in the Civil War? _____

_____

3. Who led the Confederate army? _____

_____

4. Who led the Union army? _____

_____

5. How did women help during the Civil War? _____

_____

6. What were Abraham Lincoln's goals after the Civil War? _____

_____

Think and Apply

Sequencing Events   Write the numbers **1, 2, 3, 4,** and **5** next to these sentences to show the correct order.

_____ In 1863 President Lincoln gave orders that slaves in the Confederate States were free.

_____ In 1861 Confederate soldiers attacked Fort Sumter.

_____ President Lincoln was killed after the war ended.

_____ Robert E. Lee surrendered to Ulysses S. Grant.

_____ In 1865 the Union captured the Confederate capital at Richmond.

Journal Writing

Write a paragraph about the Civil War in your journal. Tell how it began or how it ended. Write at least five sentences.

Skill Builder

Reading a Table   A **table** lists a group of facts. You can compare facts by reading tables. Look at the table below. To learn facts about the North and the South, read the numbers listed beneath each heading. Read the table from left to right to find out what the numbers in the table stand for. Use the table to answer each question.

THE NORTH AND SOUTH BEFORE THE CIVIL WAR		
	North	South
Money	$330,000,000	$47,000,000
Number of factories and shops	111,000	21,000
Miles of railroad track	22,000	9,000

1. How much money did the North have? _____

_____

2. How many factories and shops did the South have? _____

_____

3. How many miles of railroad track did the North have? _____

_____

4. Did the North or the South have less money? _____

_____

5. Did the North or the South have more factories and shops? _____

_____

6. Did the North or the South have more miles of railroad track? _____

_____

Study the time line on this page. Then use the words in blue print to finish the story. Write the words you choose on the correct blank lines.

slaves	Abe Lincoln	state
Texas	California	Lee
Cession	Confederate	Civil War

In 1836 _____ won a war for independence from Mexico.

In 1845 Texas became a _____ . The United States fought

a war with Mexico. From that war the United States got the Mexican

_____ . After the gold rush, _____ became

a state in 1850.

As the nation grew larger, the North and the South quarreled about slavery.

In 1861 southern states started a new nation called the _____

States of America. Later that year, the _____ began. In 1863

President Lincoln said that _____ in the Confederate States were

free. In 1865 General _____ surrendered to General Grant. The

North had won. A few days later, _____ was killed.

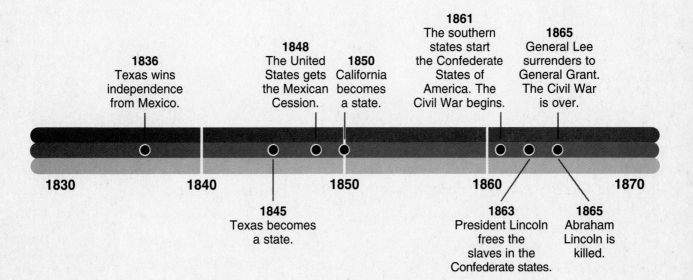

1836
Texas wins
independence
from Mexico.

1848
The United
States gets
the Mexican
Cession.

1850
California
becomes
a state.

1861
The southern
states start
the Confederate
States of
America. The
Civil War begins.

1865
General Lee
surrenders to
General Grant.
The Civil War
is over.

1830   1840   1850   1860   1870

1845
Texas becomes
a state.

1863
President Lincoln
frees the
slaves in the
Confederate states.

1865
Abraham
Lincoln is
killed.

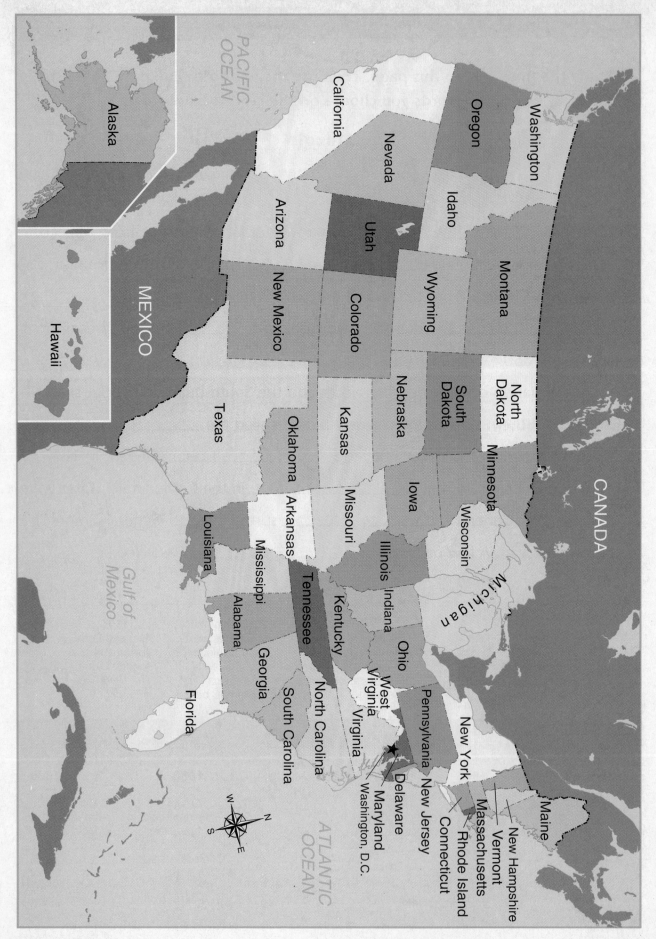

PACIFIC OCEAN

Alaska

MEXICO

Hawaii

California

Oregon

Washington

Nevada

Idaho

Montana

Arizona

Utah

Wyoming

North Dakota

New Mexico

Colorado

South Dakota

Minnesota

Texas

Oklahoma

Kansas

Nebraska

Iowa

Wisconsin

Louisiana

Arkansas

Missouri

Illinois

Indiana

Michigan

CANADA

Gulf of Mexico

Mississippi

Tennessee

Kentucky

Ohio

West Virginia

Alabama

Georgia

South Carolina

North Carolina

Virginia

Pennsylvania

New York

Florida

Delaware

Maryland

Washington, D.C.

New Jersey

Connecticut

Rhode Island

Massachusetts

Vermont

New Hampshire

Maine

ATLANTIC OCEAN

W N S E

amendments page 55
Amendments are laws that are added to the Constitution.

American Revolution page 43
The American Revolution was the war that the American colonies fought against Great Britain. It started in 1775 and ended in 1781.

Bill of Rights page 55
The Bill of Rights is the first ten amendments that were added to the Constitution.

body of water page 32
A body of water is a large area of water. Lakes and oceans are bodies of water.

border page 85
A border is a line that separates one state from another. A border can also separate cities, towns, and countries.

Boston Tea Party page 42
During the Boston Tea Party, Americans went on three British tea ships. They threw all the tea into the ocean because they did not want to pay for the tea.

boundaries page 66
Boundaries are the lines around a city, state, or country. Rivers, oceans, and mountains can be boundaries. Boundaries are often shown as lines drawn on maps.

buffalo page 5
A buffalo is an ox. It is a large animal with horns and fur.

capital page 54
The capital of a country is the city where the government meets.

capture page 79
To capture means to take and hold a person, place, or thing by using force.

Catholics page 17
Catholics are people who believe in the Christian religion. The pope is the leader of the Catholic religion.

Church of England page 20
Church of England means all the churches in England that accept the king of England as the head of the church.

citizens page 108
Citizens are members of a country.

Civil War page 126
The Civil War was the war fought between the North and the South. The war was fought between 1861 and 1865.

claimed page 12
When a country claimed land, it meant it would own and rule that land.

coast page 114
The coast is land along the ocean.

colony page 25
A colony is land that is ruled by another nation.

commander in chief page 64
The commander in chief is the most important leader of the army.

Confederates page 125
The people of the Confederate States of America were called Confederates.

Confederate States of America page 122
Eleven southern states left the United States and started their own country. The new country was called the Confederate States of America.

Congress page 53
Congress is all the people in the United States Senate and House of Representatives who write laws for the nation.

constitution page 52
A constitution is a set of laws. The United States Constitution is a set of laws for the United States.

cotton page 5
Cotton is a plant that is used to make cloth. You can wear clothes made of cotton.

covered wagons page 113
Covered wagons are wagons that are covered with heavy cloth and pulled by horses or other animals. People traveled west in covered wagons.

crops page 73
Crops are plants grown by farmers. Corn and cotton are two kinds of crops.

Declaration of Independence page 46
The Declaration of Independence was an important paper that said the American colonies were a free nation.

destroy page 127
To destroy means to break and to ruin. A war can destroy homes, farms, and cities.

disabilities page 92
People with disabilities are less able to do certain things. Not being able to see is a disability.

doubled page 74
When the United States doubled in size, it became twice as large as it had been in 1776.

education page 92
Education means the things you learn from school and from different people and places.

electric sparks page 59
Electric sparks are tiny bits of electricity that give off small amounts of light for a few seconds.

equal page 46
People who are equal have the same importance.

escape page 121
To escape means to become free by leaving a person, place, or thing.

First Lady page 65
The wife of the President of the United States is called the First Lady.

fort page 102
A fort is a building from which an army can fight its enemies.

freedom of religion page 20
Freedom of religion means you can pray the way you want to pray.

freedom of the press page 54
Freedom of the press means you can write what you want to write in newspapers and books.

freedom of the seas page 79
Freedom of the seas means that ships can go wherever they want to go.

Gadsden Purchase page 108
The United States bought land from Mexico called the Gadsden Purchase.

general page 47
A general is an important army leader.

goal page 127
A goal is something a person wants and tries to get.

gold rush page 116
A gold rush is a time when many people move into an area in order to find gold.

governor page 21
A governor is a government leader for a state, town, or area.

House of Representatives page 53
The House of Representatives is one of the two houses, or parts, of Congress. It has 435 members.

in debt page 27
A person who is in debt owes money to other people.

independent page 46
An independent country rules itself. It is not ruled by another country.

judge page 54
Judges are people who rule on cases in court.

Louisiana Purchase page 74
The Louisiana Purchase was the sale of a large piece of land west of the Mississippi River. The United States bought it from France in 1803.

Loyalists page 47
Loyalists were Americans who did not want the colonies to become independent. They helped Great Britain during the American Revolution.

manage page 63
To manage means to control and take care of something.

Manifest Destiny page 106
Manifest Destiny was the idea that the United States should rule all land from the Atlantic Ocean to the Pacific Ocean.

Mayflower Compact page 21
The Mayflower Compact was the Pilgrims' plan for ruling themselves in America.

Mexican Cession page 108
The land that the United States won during the Mexican War was called the Mexican Cession.

missions page 17
Missions are places where people teach others how to become Christians.

nation page 40
A nation is a large group of people living together in one country.

navy page 80
The navy is a nation's warships and all the people who work on the warships.

New World page 12
People in Europe called North America and South America the New World because they had not known about these continents.

Oregon Trail page 114
The trail that wagons followed through the West to Oregon was called the Oregon Trail.

oxen page 113
An ox is an animal like a cow. Oxen is the word used for more than one ox.

Parliament page 41
All the people who are chosen to write the laws for Great Britain and the building they work in are called Parliament.

pass page 116
A pass is a trail through the mountains.

peace treaty page 22
A peace treaty is an agreement not to fight.

plantations page 120
Plantations are very large farms where crops like cotton and tobacco are grown.

port page 42
A port is a place on an ocean or river where ships are loaded and unloaded.

priests page 17
Priests are people who lead religious services and teach about the Catholic religion.

printer page 58
A printer is a person who prints books and newspapers.

printing shop page 58
A printing shop is a place with machines for printing books and newspapers.

products page 121
Products are things that are made by people or by nature. Shoes are a factory product. Apples are a natural product.

property page 109
All the land and other things you own are your property.

public schools page 92
Public schools are schools that are paid for with tax money. You do not pay to study in a public school.

publish page 58
To publish means to prepare a book or newspaper so it can be sold.

quarrel page 119
To quarrel means to argue or not agree about something.

rebuild page 128
To rebuild means to build something again.

religion page 4
Religion is the way people believe in and pray to God or to many gods.

religious page 26
Religious means having to do with religion.

representatives page 53
People who make laws in the House of Representatives are called representatives.

republic page 103
A republic is a country where people vote for their leaders. These leaders make laws for the people and lead the government.

Senate page 53
The Senate is one of the two houses, or parts, of Congress. It has 100 members.

senators page 53
People who make laws in the Senate are senators.

settlers page 25
Settlers are people who come to live in a new place.

short cut page 31
A short cut is a shorter way to go to a place.

slavery page 15
Slavery means people being owned by other people. Slaves were forced to work without pay.

snowshoes page 33
Snowshoes are wooden frames that you attach to your shoes. They help you walk on deep snow.

spices page 10
Spices are added to food to improve the way it tastes and smells.

Stamp Act page 41
The Stamp Act said that Americans in the British colonies had to pay a tax on things like newspapers.

subjects page 94
The courses that you study in school, such as math and science, are subjects.

sugar cane page 120
We get most of our sugar from the tall plant called sugar cane.

Supreme Court page 54
The Supreme Court is the highest court. It decides if laws agree with the Constitution.

surrender page 64
To surrender in a war means to give up, stop fighting, and agree that your side has lost.

tariffs page 88
Tariffs are taxes on goods from other countries.

tax page 41
Tax is money that you must pay to the government.

Texas Revolution page 103
The war that Texans fought to win their independence from Mexico was the Texas Revolution.

tobacco page 26
Tobacco is a plant. The leaves of this plant are smoked in pipes, cigars, and cigarettes.

Trail of Tears page 88
The trip that Native Americans were forced to make to the West was called the Trail of Tears.

Union page 125
The Union is the United States.

wagon train page 113
Covered wagons that traveled together on a trail formed a wagon train.